# NATIVE AMERICAN
# GARDENING

Every little thing
is sent for something,
and in that thing
there should be happiness
and the power to make happy.
Like the grasses
showing tender faces to each other,
this we should do.

—Black Elk
*Black Elk Speaks*

# Native American
# GARDENING

## Stories, Projects and Recipes
## for Families

Michael J. Caduto and Joseph Bruchac

Interior Illustrations by
Mary Adair
Adelaide Murphy Tyrol
and Carol Wood

Foreword by Gary Paul Nabhan
Preface by Marjorie Waters

Fulcrum Publishing
Golden, Colorado

Library of Congress Cataloging-in-Publication Data
    Caduto, Michael J.
        Native American gardening : stories, projects and recipes for families / by Michael
    J. Caduto and Joseph Bruchac.
            p.    cm.
        Includes bibliographical references and index.
        ISBN 1-55591-148-X (pbk.)
        1. Indians of North America—Agriculture. 2. Gardening—North America. 3. Indians of North America—Folklore.  4. Indian cookery—North America.  I. Bruchac, Joseph, 1942–  . II. Title.
    E98.A3C24  1996
    635'.089'975—dc20                                                          95–47301
                                                                                CIP

Printed in Canada
0   9   8   7   6   5

Fulcrum Publishing
16100 Table Mountain Parkway, Suite 300 • Golden, Colorado 80403
(800) 992-2908 • (303) 277-1623
www.fulcrum-books.com

# Permissions

## Permission to reprint the following is gratefully acknowledged:

The quote by Black Elk that appears on page ii is from John G. Neihardt's *Black Elk Speaks* (1972) and is reprinted with permission of the University of Nebraska Press, Lincoln, Nebraska.

The map, "Native North America" on pages xvi-xvii, showing the locations of Native North American cultures and culture regions, is printed with permission of Michael J. Caduto (© 1996). Cartography by Stacy Miller, Upper Marlboro, Maryland.

The photographs that appear on pages xv, 11, 23, 43, 119, 124 and 132 by John Running (© 1996) are reprinted with his permission.

The quote by Maxidiwiac (Buffalo Bird Woman) (page 4), the description of a traditional Hidatsa garden (pages 88–94), the description of a Hidatsa scarecrow (pages 104–5) and the recipe for making "Hidatsa Four-Vegetables Mixed" (page 134) are adapted with permission from Gilbert L. Wilson's *Buffalo Bird Woman's Garden* (1987), published by the Minnesota Historical Society Press, Saint Paul, Minnesota.

The quote by Sevenka Qoyawayma that appears on pages 4–5 is from Polingaysi Qoyawayma's *No Turning Back* (1964), as told to Vada F. Carlson, and is reprinted with permission from the University of New Mexico Press, Albuquerque, New Mexico.

The photographs on pages 7, 74 and 77 by Charles Mann (© 1996) are reprinted with his permission.

The photographs that appear on page 9 (by Ted Curtin) and page 53 are reprinted here with permission of Plimoth Plantation, Inc., Plymouth, Massachusetts, U.S.A. (© 1996).

The photographs that appear on pages 16, 36, 55, 71, 82, 96, 101, 127, 129, 135 and 138 by Michael J. Caduto (© 1996) are reprinted with his permission.

The photographs that appear on pages 20 (© 1972), 65 (© 1964) and 68 (© 1989) by Alexander Lowry are reprinted here with his permission.

The section called "Understanding and Appreciating Other Cultures" that appears on pages 21–23 is adapted with permission from material produced by the Institute for American Indian Studies, 38 Curtis Road, P.O. Box 1260, Washington, Connecticut 06793.

The lists of ideas for "Choosing a Site" and "Choosing Seeds," found on pages 31 and 42, are adapted from Eliot Coleman's *The New Organic Grower: Revised and Expanded Edition* (1995), and are used here with permission from Chelsea Green Publishing Co., White River Junction, Vermont.

The activities describing how to make a compost pile, how to measure rainfall and how to make manure tea, found on pages 40, 48 and 50, are adapted from Marjorie Waters's *The Victory Garden Kids' Book* (1994) and are used here with permission from the author and the Globe Pequot Press, Old Saybrook, Connecticut.

The photograph of the full moon that appears on page 46 is used with permission, © University of California Regents; UCO/Lick Observatory image.

The quote by Onondaga Chief Louis Farmer that appears on page 70 is from Steve Wall and Harvey Arden's *Wisdomkeepers* (1990) and is reprinted with permission from Beyond Words Publishing, Inc., Hillsboro, Oregon.

The photograph on page 80 by Dale S. Turner (© 1996) is reprinted with his permission.

The description of a traditional Wampanoag Three Sisters Garden, on pages 81–88, is used with permission of the late Nanepashemet, member of the Assonet Band of the Wampanoag Nation and Research Associate at the Plimoth Plantation, Inc., Plymouth, Massachusetts, U.S.A.

The chart of "Gourd Birdhouse Specifications" on page 100 is adapted from Verne E. Davison's *Attracting Birds: From the Great Plains to the Atlantic*, © 1967 by Verne E. Davison, and is reprinted with permission of HarperCollins Publishers, Inc., New York.

The "Pueblo Corn-Grinding Song" on page 117, the recipes called "Plains Corn Bread" (page 126), "Southwestern Kneeldown Bread" (page 126), "Coal-Roasted Corn" (page 126), "Hot Coal Squash" (page 131), "Pueblo Succotash" (page 133) and "Indian Pudding" (page 134) are adapted from Darcy Williamson and Lisa Railsback's *Cooking with Spirit: North American Indian Food and Fact* (1988) and are used with permission of Darcy Williamson.

The photograph on page 118 by Alan C. Graham (© 1996) is reprinted with his permission.

The recipes called "Corn Chowder" (page 126), "Johnnycakes" (page 127), "Hominy Grits" (page 128), "Yellow Squash Soup" (page 131) and "Sunflower Seed Cakes" (page 136) are adapted from Barrie Kavasch's *Native Harvests: Recipes and Botanicals of the American Indian* (1979), published by Random House/Vintage Books, New York, and are used with permission of the author.

The recipe for "Johnnycakes" on page 127 is used with permission, courtesy Dr. Ella W. T. Sekatau of the Narragansett Indian Nation.

The recipes for "Tortillas" (page 128) and "Corn Drink" (Atol de Elote) (page 135) are adapted from *Comida Guatemalteca: Guatemalan Food* (1988) by Guatemalan Women Refugees, published by Pro Guatemalan Children, Seattle, Washington, and are used with permission.

The recipes for "Refried Beans" (page 130), "Quechan (Yuman) Squash" (page 131), "Taos Pumpkin" (page 132), "Fried Squash Blossoms" (page 132), "Havasupai Squash-Blossom Corn Pudding" (page 133) "and "Roasted Pumpkin or Squash Seeds" (page 135) are adapted from Carolyn Niethammer's *American Indian Food and Lore: 150 Authentic Recipes* (copyright © 1974 by Carolyn Niethammer), used with permission of Macmillan Publishing USA, a Simon & Schuster/Macmillan Company.

The adaptation of the recipe for "Bean Bread" on page 130 is used with permission from Frances Gwaltney's *Corn Recipes from the Indians* (1988), published by Cherokee Publications, Cherokee, North Carolina.

The "Cherokee Butterbean Game" on page 138 is adapted with permission from Paul B. Hamel and Mary U. Chiltoskey's *Cherokee Plants—Their Uses: A 400 Year History,* published by Cherokee Publications, Cherokee, North Carolina.

The photograph on page 157 by John Sheldon (© 1996 by Michael J. Caduto) is used here with his permission.

The activities and information throughout this book by Michael J. Caduto (© 1996) are reprinted with his permission.

The stories by Joseph Bruchac throughout this book are reprinted with his permission.

The story illustrations by Mary Adair throughout this book are reprinted with her permission.

The illustrations by Adelaide Murphy Tyrol throughout this book are reprinted with her permission.

The illustrations by Carol M. Wood that accompany the activities and information throughout this book are reprinted with her permission.

*In memory of*
*Nanepashemet*

# Contents

# Foreword

On Thanksgiving Day in 1992—during the five hundredth anniversary of Spanish arrival in the Americas—children from Pima and Maricopa tribal communities in Arizona shared a special feast. They did not eat the foods shared between the Pilgrims and Native Americans of the Eastern Seaboard. Instead, they ate what their ancestors had eaten before any European ever set his foot on the soil of the North American continent.

Among the Native foods eaten that day were the drought-hardy tepary bean, still a garden crop among the Pima; the flower buds of cholla cactus, a spiny plant grown prehistorically among the Pueblos; and the sweet flour of mesquite pods, from a bean tree that lines nearly every field of Native crops in the Southwest. Some of the foods had been harvested by the schoolchildren over the previous few weeks. Others had been donated by Pima elders, some of whom still farm the way their grandparents had taught them at the turn of the century. Still others were gifts from Native Seeds/SEARCH, a crop conservation organization now directed by an O'odham man who is a relative of the Pima children. Whatever the immediate source of these foods was, the ultimate sources were the Earth itself, the ancient farming traditions of Native Americans and the Circle of Life, which includes all plants and animals.

There is hope that the Gila River Pima children may benefit directly from the seeds their ancestors safeguarded, through maintaining a diet rich in nutrition and high in fiber. Without such Native foods in their diet and without the kind of exercise that gardening can give them, these children may become as vulnerable to a nutrition-related disease as their parents have been. Over the last half century, as Native foods were replaced in their parents' diet by store-bought foods of poor nutritional value, the older

*Some Native foods of the Southwest (from top to bottom): tepary beans, flower bud of the cholla cactus and mesquite pods.*

generation began to suffer from diabetes. In fact, a greater percentage of Pima adults have had their health damaged by the loss of Native foods and the rise in diabetes than any ethnic community in the world.

Now, some young Pima children have begun to grow Native crops in their gardens and to eat wild foods from the lands surrounding their home, in hopes that this will prevent them from ever suffering from diabetes. They are not the only children gardening with Native crop seeds and learning the lore of these plants from elders. When Danny Pablo, a Tohono O'odham child, was five, he learned to farm Native beans, devil's claw and squashes, following his grandfather around his fields like a "little shadow" of the elder farmer. Now he is a teenager and has had to take over his own family's garden, for his father passed away a few years ago. But the echoes of his father's and grandfather's words still guide how he grows his garden. He combines ancient seeds with new tools such as rototillers and chicken wire to keep his desert garden healthy, well tended and protected.

Children from other cultures also benefit from the Native American agricultural legacy in many ways. Kanin Routson lives on a farm in a valley surrounded by mountains, where his family grows almost all their own food except for the grain they purchase from a food co-op. Each brief summer, it rains in the mountains above the valley, but few showers fall on the Routson farm before frosts begin to come again. By growing fast-maturing, hardy sunflowers, black beans and blue corn from the Hopi and other tribes who live in similarly harsh climates, Kanin has had relatively good success in his own garden over the last four years. He was recently introduced to several Native American elders—including a 106-year-old woman who grew up on Native foods in a comparably extreme climate—who give him additional inspiration to continue with his love of Native plants.

Michael J. Caduto and Joseph Bruchac give us helpful hints on how to be better gardeners, but their stories also remind us that none of us can make it on our own—we are part of the Circle of Life, which includes beneficial insects, migratory pollinators and nitrogen-fixing bacteria. They are as critical to an abundant harvest as we are. The stories and prayers of Native American farming traditions remind us of these connections. In fact, they also remind us that stories which exclude plants and animals are poor, just as a soil without earthworms is considered poor. We are all enriched by the many lives that inhabit the stories retold to us by Joseph and Michael, for they help us remember where our food comes from—historically, physically, ecologically and spiritually. Let us all try to carry these stories and seeds on to future generations, who may need them just as desperately as we do.

—Gary Paul Nabhan, Ph.D.
Native Seeds/SEARCH cofounder

# Acknowledgments

## From the Authors:

The work of many hands has brought this book to you, the reader. Our gratitude goes out to Bob Baron, Publisher; Carmel Huestis, Editor; Patty Maher, Production Manager; and to all those at Fulcrum Publishing who were involved in the various stages of editing, design, production and marketing who have helped this book reach the hearts and hands of those who care about gardening. We are indebted to the artists for enriching these pages with their beautiful images. The stories are illustrated by Mary Adair. The balance of the illustrations, by Adelaide Murphy Tyrol and Carol Wood, can be distinguished by Adelaide Tyrol's initials. The photographers, too, including Ted Curtin, Alan C. Graham, Alexander Lowry, Charles Mann, John Running, John Sheldon and Dale S. Turner, have helped these pages come to life. Our sincere thanks to Gary Paul Nabhan, Ph.D., and Marjorie Waters for taking time out of their busy schedules to write the thoughtful foreword and preface, respectively.

## From Michael J. Caduto:

My deepest thanks to Joseph Bruchac for contributing these beautiful stories, which bring such meaning, connectedness and good humor to this book, and for his contribution of the glossary and the section on storytelling. I am grateful for the gift of sharing from Nanepashemet, member of the Assonet Band of the Wampanoag Nation, who was instrumental as I researched a traditional Wampanoag garden and put those ideas to work in my own garden over the past few summers. Nanepashemet, after a prolonged illness, did not live to see this book in print. His kind heart and good humor will be greatly missed. I have been touched by the gifts from Maxidiwiac, "Buffalo Bird Woman," who lived long ago and left a rich legacy of traditional Hidatsa gardening. Thank you to the Haudenosaunee, the People of the Longhouse, for the great gift of the "Three Sisters Garden," and to all Native gardeners throughout North America.

This book has been greatly strengthened by the observant, expert reading performed by these major reviewers as I worked toward the final draft, and to whom I owe a great debt: Kevin Dahl, Associate Director, Native Seeds/ SEARCH; Kathy Henderson, host of *Kathy Henderson's Garden,* WQXI-AM-790, Atlanta; Elisheva Kaufman, Facilitator for Global Gardens: A Program for Schoolwide Gardening, Environmental Stewardship and Ecological Design; E. Barrie Kavasch, Ethnobotanist, Trustee and Research Associate of the Institute for American Indian Studies; Jenepher Lingelbach, Director of ELF

(Environmental Learning for the Future) nationwide, Vermont Institute of Natural Science; John Moody, Ethnohistorian and Independent Scholar; Gary Paul Nabhan, Ph.D., cofounder of Native Seeds/SEARCH and Science Advisor at the Arizona–Sonora Desert Museum; the late Nanepashemet, member of the Assonet Band of the Wampanoag Nation; Eve Pranis, Associate Director of Education, National Gardening Association; and Marjorie Waters, author of *The Victory Garden Kids' Book*.

With much appreciation, I would like to recall the assistance offered by all the people who field-tested the activities and recipes, and who helped in many other ways while this book was being written: Benjamin Bear, Meadowbrook Gourd Crafters; Esther Caduto; Mimi Emerson; Cecile T. Levesque; Ellen Marie Levesque; Jonathan Richard Levesque; Mildred Alice Levesque; Richard David Levesque; Suzanne Stofflet; and Kathy Wildman of Hearts & Flowers Seed Collections & Butterfly Farm, Sunbury, Ohio.

Warm thanks to my wife, Marie, for helping with ideas, moral support and field-testing. Thanks to Barbara Brainerd and the late John Brainerd, fellow lovers of children and the natural world. Finally, my appreciation to those whose love of gardening and expertise have inspired me for many years of deeply rewarding seasons of growing: my mother, Esther Caduto; Kenneth Whitman, Sr. of Coventry, Rhode Island; and Eliot Coleman, innovator, thinker and author of *The New Organic Grower: A Master's Manual of Tools and Techniques for the Home and Market Gardener*.

## From Joseph Bruchac:

Thanks to my grandfather, Jesse Bowman, who first showed me how to fit the ground to plant; to my wife, Carol, companion and fellow gardener for more than three decades; and to my two sons who have carried our caring for this Earth into another generation. *Wliwini, wli d8go w8ngan*. Thanks, to all our relations.

# Preface

Kids take eagerly to gardening: it's outdoors, it involves dirt and shovels and it offers them something close to the power of the Creator. Just watch their faces when they see a seedling in the place where they have planted a seed, or a squash gaining color every day, or a bean suddenly ready to pick.

*Native American Gardening* provides the information and proven organic procedures children need to take advantage of this enthusiasm and grow a successful garden. But it is more than a book of technique. It gives children a chance to take part in one of Native people's most basic and essential activities.

Using this book, children can grow the foods that are important to Native Americans, both spiritually and nutritionally. They can absorb wisdom that has accumulated for generations. They can hear the stories Native children hear about how and why the garden grows, stories that give gardening great richness and meaning.

There may be no better way for children to understand the Native American tradition, or learn the profound lessons it has to teach.

—Marjorie Waters
author of *The Victory Garden Kids' Book*

DAVIS STRAIT

LABRADOR
SEA

nais
pil

GULF OF
ST. LAWRENCE

MICMAC

MALISEET
PASSAMAQUODDY
ABENAKI PENOBSCOT
WABANAKI PEOPLES
PENNACOOK
MASSACHUSET
WAMPANOAG
NARRAGANSETT
Mohegan, Pequot
Munsee Shinnecock
nni Lenape
(Delaware)

Nanticoke
whatan

East Coast Algonquians

ATLANTIC

OCEAN

—→ ◄◊► NATIVE ◄◊► ←—

NORTH AMERICA
◄◊►

Lucayo

C A R I B

Carib
TAINO
Arawak
TAINO
TAINO
Carib
TAINO
Carib
B E A N

CARIBBEAN
SEA

BBEAN

ba
Cuna
Panama
Carib
aymi
Choco
Choco

Cultural areas and tribal locations of Native North Americans. This map shows tribal locations as they appeared around 1600, except for the Seminole culture in the southeast, the Tuscaroras in the northeast and the Hohokam in the Southwest. The Seminoles formed from a group which withdrew from the Muskogee (Creek) and joined with several other groups on the Georgia/Florida border to form the Seminoles, a name which has been used since about 1775. In the eastern woodlands, the Tuscaroras were admitted to the Haudenosaunee (Iroquois) League in 1722 after many refugees from the Tuscarora Wars (1711–1713) in the southeast fled northward. In the Southwest, the Hohokam occupied Pueblo Grande in what is now Phoenix, Arizona, from around A.D. 800 to around 1450.

There are hundreds of other Cultures/Nations that are not included due to limited space. The generally recognized name of at least one distinct Culture is given in each area, emphasizing those with large populations, past and/or present. Traditional names are used where possible because many names in general use are not preferred by Native North Americans.

*And so it is to this day ... the people sing and dance those songs of thanksgiving to the Corn.*

Chapter 1

# *Introduction*
# Native Gardens and the
# Circle of Life

## Onenha, The Corn
### *(Tuscarora—Northeast)*

There was a man, long ago, who used to travel. In those days, when people walked upon the trails, they would sometimes lose from their packs a few seeds of corn or squash or beans. Most people paid no attention to those stray seeds where they fell, but it was not so with this man. It was his custom, whenever he saw a corn seed or a bean seed or a squash seed on the trail, to stop and pick it up and speak to it.

"My friend," he would say to the seed, "I see that you are in need. I will take care of you."

One day, when this man was far from home, he became ill. He knew no one near the place where he had made his small camp, a little lodge made of bent saplings covered with bark. So there was no one who could help him. Though it grew colder, he was too weak to make a fire and he could not get food for himself. He lay there in his small lodge with his robe pulled up over his head, certain that he would soon die of starvation.

One night as he lay there, though, he began to hear the voices of two women speaking just outside his rough lodge.

"What shall we do?" said the voice of the first woman. "This man is very ill and in need of help."

"It is right that we should help him," said the voice of the second woman. "Many times he helped us and our sisters when we'd fallen upon the trail and were in distress."

Hearing those words, the man uncovered his head and sat up, thinking he would see those women who were talking. But when he looked around, there was no one there.

1

The next night, once again, he heard those two women talking. Just as before, he uncovered his head to look, but no one was there. And on the third night that same thing happened once again. On the fourth night, though, it was different. On that night the man had a dream. In his dream a small woman with long hair appeared to him. She was very beautiful. When she spoke to him her voice was like the singing of the wind among the cornstalks.

"I have been asked to come to you," the woman said, "to tell you we have decided to help you. Many times as you walked on the trails, you saw my sisters or myself, the seeds of corn and beans and squash, lost and fallen upon the Earth. Whenever you saw us, you always picked us up, called us your friend and said you would take care of us. That is why I have been sent to help you. This is what you must do to grow well again. When the rain falls, place a cup where it will fill with rain. Drink that rainwater. It is a medicine and will cure your illness."

The small woman paused, but the man said nothing. He only listened until she spoke again.

"There will come a time," she said, "when you will hear us singing in the fields, giving thanks that you are well again and traveling over the Earth. Know that there are certain times when we sing and dance in that way. The first time is when we sprout from the Earth after planting. We sing and dance in thanksgiving at that time. The next time that we sing and dance is when the people hoe the ground around us, giving our roots room to grow. The third time we sing and dance is the time of second hoeing. We also sing and dance at the time when the people pick the ears of corn to husk them, braid them together in the fields and hang them on the frames to dry. The last time that we sing and dance is when those ears of corn are carried into the lodges. Each of those times we sing and we dance the Corn Dance.

"You must tell the people that they, too, must sing and dance at those times to show us that they are pleased to see us growing and coming again into their lodges. If they sing and dance the Corn Songs, then we will always continue to provide the people with what they need."

So the little Corn Woman spoke to him in his dream. The man listened carefully, remembering all that she said. When he woke the next morning, he heard the rain falling on the roof of his lodge. He made a small cup of bark and pushed it outside so that the rain filled it. He was so weak he could barely lift that cup. But as soon as he drank the rainwater, he felt his strength begin to return and his illness start to leave him.

That night, as he lay there on the floor of his small lodge, he heard a sound coming from above him. He looked up at the drying pole which he had placed across the top of his lodge. It had been empty before, but now strings of corn hung from the drying pole. Those strings of corn were swinging gently back and forth, and the sound of singing was coming from them. Looking closely at those ears of corn, he could see the faces of women in them and he began to understand the songs they sang. One of the songs went like this:

> Among the flowers
> I am singing and dancing
> Among the flowers
> I am singing and dancing

Each of the songs was like that, a beautiful melody, which the man knew was a song he had to learn so that he and his people could sing it to give thanks to the Corn. By the time all of the songs had been sung, the man knew them all and he was completely well again.

When the next day came, the man set forth again on his travels. He returned to his own people and told them about all that had happened. He sang to the Council of Elders the songs which the Corn Woman taught him.

The Council of Elders listened closely to all the man said. Then the Elders announced to all the people that it was a good thing those songs had been given to the people. "These new songs," the elders said, "shall be sung when the next season of planting comes."

When the time came for the first spouts of corn to come from the ground, that man heard the sound of singing coming from the fields. He looked into the fields and there he saw the Corn People dancing. There were many of them, women and girls. As they danced, they swayed slowly and gently, just as the cornstalks do in the wind. He listened closely, knowing those songs of thanksgiving should always be sung by his people from that time on. He knew that when those songs were sung, his people should dance as the Corn People dance.

And so it is to this day. From the time when the first green shoots appear in the fields to the time when the strings of corn are bought into the lodges, the people sing and dance those songs of thanksgiving to the Corn.

## Native Gardens and the Circle of Life

We cared for our corn in those days as we would care for a child; for we Indian people loved our gardens, just as a mother loves her children; and we thought that our growing corn liked to hear us sing, just as children like to hear their mother sing to them.[1]

—Maxidiwiac (Buffalo Bird Woman)

*Hidatsa*

The man in the story of "Onenha, The Corn" is sick and weak with hunger. He is in need of something to heal him. He begins to get well when the spirit of Corn Woman speaks to him in a dream and tells him to drink rainwater. Rainwater becomes the medicine that cures his illness.

Later, this man hears music coming from the corn that is hanging from the drying pole in the lodge overhead. He sees women's faces singing from those ears of corn. These are the songs that Corn Woman says the people must sing and dance when the corn is planted, as it grows and is harvested. To this day, the Tuscarora receive the gift of corn because they sing and dance the songs of Thanksgiving.

Those faces that appear in the ears of corn, and the songs they sing, are calling to all of us. They remind us that beyond the physical work of the garden lies the need to care for Earth, to celebrate and to sing and dance in thanksgiving for the corn and all the gifts of life we receive. The circle of giving and receiving is found throughout Native North America.

Mother Corn has fed you, as she has fed all Hopi people, since long, long ago when she was no larger than my thumb. Mother corn is a promise of food and life. I grind with gratitude for the richness of our harvest, not with cross feelings of working too hard. As I kneel at my grinding stone, I bow my head in prayer, thanking the great forces for provision. I have received much. I am willing to give much in return ... there must always be a giving back for what one receives.[2]

—Sevenka Qoyawayma
*Hopi*

A garden, in Native North America, is not just a place to grow food. Taking care of a garden is one of the most important ways that people become a part of the great Circles of Life. Every time we plant a seed, add compost to the soil, water a seedling, pull a weed, talk or sing gently to the plants or say "thank you" for the blooming flowers, we are giving a gift. In turn we receive knowledge, peace of mind, food for our bodies, a growing spirit of giving and a sense of having full life.

When we give this kind of close attention to plants, we really begin to know them—their habits and the changes they experience. We notice the plants' enemies and problems as soon as they begin to attack, such as insects, diseases, drought and other stresses. We see when the plants are doing well, and when they are not.

Although this book is about Native American gardening, it is important to remember that nature itself is a wild garden. Gardening grew out of the age-old practice of gathering wild edibles from the natural world. Cultivated gardening began when people first selected the crops and planted the seeds of wild plants that were most desirable. An ancient Abenaki custom, for example, uses squirrels to plant nut trees. In springtime the Abenaki put piles of acorns and butternuts out for the squirrels who live around their home and village. The squirrels become tree planters: they gather and bury the nuts in the ground for their food stores, but do not remember where all the seeds are buried.

*Squirrels are one of Nature's gardeners.*

# Seeds of Life

Although the man in "Onenha, The Corn" listens well to the advice of Corn Woman, he is truly saved by the compassion and caring he showed toward the seeds of the *Three Sisters*. This is the name used by the *Haudenosaunee*, the "People of the Longhouse" (Iroquois), to refer to the Native traditional garden of corn, beans and squash. Over the years, the man picked up the seeds that others had dropped and said to each seed, "My friend, I see that you are in need. So I will take care of you." By doing this he saves his own life. When he falls ill, the Three Sisters decide to save him because they remember how he cared for them in the past.

*If we take care of the seeds, they will take care of us.* In nature, seeds do not need the kind of care that garden seeds must have. Certain lupine seeds that were found frozen in arctic soil, for instance, sprouted when planted, even though they were more than ten thousand years old! But garden crops have come to *depend* on people to grow them. We must plant and care for the seeds if these plants are to survive.

Seed storage has helped Native Americans survive for thousands of years. Many eastern cultures stored seeds in bark-lined pits that were often dug in the floor of special lodges where the seeds could be protected from mice and other animals. The traditional farmers of the Tohono O'odham in the Southwest stored seeds from many plant varieties that could grow in different kinds of weather. Each clay "seed pot" or *olla* had a narrow neck closed with a wedge that was sealed in place with *lac,* a kind of glue. Seeds were packed in that way to protect them from insects, small animals and the weather. These seeds were stored in cool, dry caves or rock crevices near the fields and could still grow after ten years or more. If, for example, bad weather shortened the growing season, the village may have needed to plant a certain variety of seed, perhaps for a fast-growing crop of corn. These people would collect the seeds of this kind of corn from where they were stored and then grow them.[3]

## The First Garden Seeds

Many of today's modern garden crops and fruit were first grown six thousand to seven thousand years ago by the Incas of Peru, the Maya of Central America and the Aztecs of Mexico.

These cultures were the first to grow more than 150 species of plants such as corn, beans, certain varieties of squash, peanuts, peppers and tomatoes. Among these species are hundreds of different varieties, including more than 150 varieties and colors of corn.[4] Some squashes, however, originated in what is now the eastern United States, including the summer squashes, such as the scallop and crookneck squash, acorn squashes and many familiar ornamental gourds. Roughly seventy-five thousand kinds of plants have some edible parts, and Native peoples of the world have used seventy thousand of these for food at one time or another.[5] Varieties of maize (corn), beans and squash are the most important traditional garden crops in North America.

## Useful Plants of Native Origin

Native gardeners have grown many kinds of seeds and crops over the years, including sunflower, maize, squash, pumpkin, pepper, common bean, tepary bean, lima bean, tropical jack bean, chili, tomato, potato, wild rice, sweet potato, amaranth, Jerusalem artichoke, persimmon, avocado, peanut, little barley, vanilla,

*Many modern varieties of corn, squash and other crops were first grown in Central and South America.*

chocolate, cotton and tobacco.[6,7] Three out of every four plants we eat today were first grown by Native North and South Americans.[8]

During the Europeans' early years in North America, their survival depended on Native plants and the farming skills of Native North Americans. When they arrived on what is now called Cape Cod in November 1620, the Plymouth colonists found corn stored in pits. The colonists stole this seed corn and ate it to survive their first winter. In March of the following spring, a Wampanoag man named Squanto showed the colonists how to plant corn. Later, the colonists learned how to grow beans and squash, including pumpkins, in their gardens. Similarly, Native Americans gave to European arrivals and westward migrants many times over the next two hundred years.

## Keeping the Circle Strong

Inside every seed is a kind of genetic memory that goes back millions of years and helps that type of plant survive. Seeds remember how to grow plants, for example, that can live through a drought and resist being eaten or killed by insects and disease. Each kind of plant is more likely to survive if there are many different varieties of the plant that can live in different conditions. A *community* of plants is better able to adapt to changes in the environment if it contains a high level of *diversity*—a rich variety of species of plants. The number of different kinds of plants living today is called the plant world's biological diversity, or *biodiversity*.

Some Native North Americans still use plants for food, medicine, housing and other purposes. These traditional people follow the old ways with plants in the Circle of Life—they harvest thousands of Native varieties of edible plants from their gardens and in the wild places. By taking care of the many varieties of plants, they help the plants remember how to survive.

### A Broken Circle

Most of our plant food today comes from twenty of the most common crops, including corn, wheat, rye, rice and millet. Nowadays, farmers tend to grow just a few varieties of plants. These crops have not been developed for taste and nutrition, but instead because they look nice and last long and

therefore can be sent from the farm to markets around the world. Today's attractive grains and produce are easier to sell and can be stored or kept on the shelf for a long time without spoiling. Varieties grown for market and for long-distance shipping are not usually the best for the home garden.

The few crops that we grow do not tend to have the best flavor or nutritional value. These plants are not as hardy when faced with insects, diseases, drought, harsh weather and different types of soils. They often need chemical fertilizers and pesticides in order to survive. These chemicals pollute the air, water and soil and are bad for the environment.

Such a small number of crops is now being grown that, since 1900, more than half of the world's varieties of the twenty most important food crops have disappeared, including strains of rice, wheat, corn, oats, potatoes, peas and beans. In the United States, during that same span of time, over 80 percent of our varieties of flowers, fruits and vegetables have died out.[9] Local heirloom varieties are also being lost in Italy and other European countries.[10]

All around the world, more than three species of plants are becoming extinct every hour. This adds up to twenty-seven thousand species each year! The main reason for this rate of extinction

*Native North Americans use plants for many purposes besides gardening. Two dwellings, called wetus or wigwams, can be seen behind the men and women working in this traditional Wampanoag garden. Poles made from saplings support both dwellings. The wigwam on the left is protected by cattail mats, while the one on the right is covered with tree bark.*

is that the world's population is always growing, and each of us needs something from the environment in order to live. Plants disappear because of the loss of homes or *habitat,* the introduction of exotic species and alien diseases, overcollecting from the wild, poaching, and pollution of soil, water and air.[11]

Every time a plant dies out, nature forgets what that plant had "learned" and "remembered" in order to live. Biodiversity grows ever smaller and it becomes harder for people to find the kinds of plants they need to survive. An excellent book on this subject is *The Vanishing Feast: How Dwindling Genetic Diversity Threatens the World's Food Supply* by Dorothy Hinshaw Patent (New York: Harcourt Brace, 1994).

## Restoring the Circle

We are all connected in the great Circle of Life—people, plants and animals from every culture and environment. It is not too late to relearn how we are related and to begin living in ways that support the Circle and keep it strong. Gardening is an important and ancient way of being part of the Circle.

*If we take care of the seeds, they will take care of us.* The first step begins with the seeds, because they carry the memory and wisdom of how to survive. Many rare and endangered varieties of seeds are being preserved in *seed banks* that have been built in many countries. Seed banks must be expanded and land needs to be preserved as habitat for Native plants.

*Gardeners of all kinds who grow Native crops often mean the difference between the survival or extinction of many traditional varieties.* Some groups are working to preserve Native seeds and crops. The Seed Saver's Exchange on Heritage Farm in Decorah, Iowa, grows and saves heirloom seeds and preserves the folklore of Native plants. This group, and another called Native Seeds/SEARCH in Tucson, Arizona, help sustain Native varieties and seeds for future planting. Both of these groups distribute seeds to gardeners, family farmers, researchers and Native peoples, especially those who live in the southwestern United States and in Mexico. Native Seeds/SEARCH runs a seed bank with more than 1,300 collections of endangered varieties of crops.

Seeds of Change in Santa Fe, New Mexico, is another organization that preserves Native seeds and crops. The hundreds of varieties available through the Seeds of Change catalog are *open pollinated*. This allows natural forces, such as birds, insects, wind and rain, to move the pollen from the male flowers to the female flowers. All crops and seeds from Seeds of Change are *certified organic*—they are grown without the use of chemical pesticides and fertilizers. These seeds are sold to gardeners all over North America.

*Hopi lima bean seeds.*

We are all, in a way, like the man in the story "Onenha, The Corn." We can satisfy our hunger and find the cure for our ills in the garden we call Earth. Gardening brings us the joys of growing our own food, improves our health and nutrition, draws us into a life lived closer to Earth and requires that we become part of the nutrient cycle of the soil. Gardening helps us support ourselves and saves energy that would have been spent moving food to our table—food that often travels thousands of miles to reach us.

The way to move well in the Circle of Life is to garden close to the natural cycles; to cultivate a wild spirit among the plants of corn, beans, squash and other crops we choose to grow. Gardening is a truly creative act by which we invite the natural world into our lives.

# Chapter 2

# Bringing This Book to Life

## Introduction

*Native American Gardening* brings the magical world of stories together with the joyful, nurturing experience of gardening. When you hear a story, a whole new world opens up in your imagination. As these stories come to life, ears of corn begin to sing, Bean Woman embraces Corn Man and Grasshopper's song helps his garden grow.

Dig into *Native American Gardening* and you will plant Native seeds, taste freshly picked greens and vegetables, listen to the sound of bees buzzing as they pollinate squash flowers, see the rainbow colors of garden blooms and smell freshly turned earth. These stories and activities introduce you to *Three Sisters* gardening—the Native traditional garden of corn, beans and squash. *Native American Gardening* also involves you with seed preservation, natural pest control, Native diets and meals. It shows how we are all part of a global food web fed by Earth's gardens.

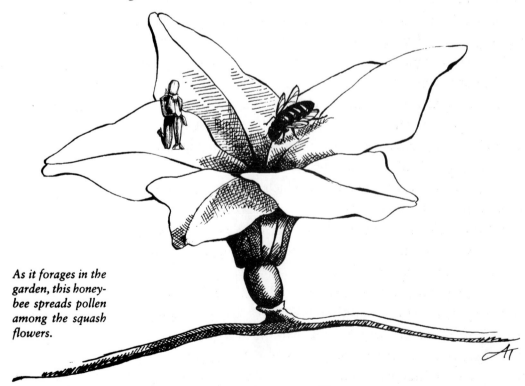

*As it forages in the garden, this honeybee spreads pollen among the squash flowers.*

These experiences immerse you in the Circles of Life through gardening. Gardens are human-made ecosystems that depend on the laws of nature. Creating a garden is like growing a meadow of edible plants. As you grow your garden, you become involved with the *cycles of nature,* such as the *solar cycle* (year), the *lunar cycle* (seasons), the *cycle of night and day* and the *water cycle.* By growing seeds and caring for the soil, you take part in the circle of life and death called the *nutrient cycle.*

*Native American Gardening* is designed to be an inspiration and a how-to manual for family experiences. It is a book for gardeners of all ages and backgrounds to share. You can use this book wherever your garden grows, whether in the backyard, in a vacant lot or on a rooftop. These stories and activities are used and enjoyed by families and children from homes in both rural and urban neighborhoods.

This book helps you understand, appreciate, care for and preserve ancient varieties of crops—the Seeds of Life. Here is your opportunity to continue the work of generations of Native North American communities of farmers who know the importance of the circle of giving and receiving with Earth. Through Native gardening and meals, stories, music, games and other activities, you will join the Circle of Celebration.

Native Americans believe that people are a part of Earth, as are the plants and animals, the air, water, rocks and sky around us. Native stories use nature to teach about relationships between people, and between people and the gardens of Earth. Native North Americans build a close relationship with nature rather than trying to control the natural world. To the Native peoples of North America, plants, animals and people are all related. This is why they care so deeply about nature and gardens.

People from every cultural tradition can renew their ties with the Circles of Life. If we look far enough into the past, we all come from traditional peoples whose lives were intertwined with the rhythms of the natural world. Native North American traditions help each of us to recall and renew those ancient ties.

Churches and other spiritual groups have been inspired by Native North American traditions that teach about Earth stewardship and deeper ties with Earth as part of Creation. Although the stories and activities come from North America, they can be adapted and used by children in other lands as well.

*In the garden we renew our connections to Earth and take part in the Circles of Life.*

## Bringing This Book to Life

Chapter 1 tells about Native North American gardens and the Circles of Life. After you finish reading Chapter 2, which describes how to use this book, go on to read Chapter 3, in which you will discover the basic, important steps that are necessary to plan and grow your garden and complete the yearly gardening cycle. The stories and activities in Chapters 4 and 5 are the heart of the book. Each "Bridges: From Legends to Life" section tells you something about the Native North American cultures that are the source of the stories. These sections are subtitled "From Legends to Life" because they explore the life lessons that come from the stories and how these relate to important ideas to consider when practicing Native gardening and preparing Native meals.

Be creative and use this book to complement your family experiences. First, have fun sharing the stories and illustrations. Then read the "Bridges: From Legends to Life" sections, which link the stories and activities. Each activity has a title and a description of what you will be doing. Then follows a list of all the materials you need for the activity. Most of the materials required for the stories and activities can be found outdoors or at home; they are simple, common and inexpensive.

When you are ready to do the activity, read over the section called "Digging In." These sections are like recipes in a cook-book—they tell you all the steps you must take to carry out the activity.

Chapters 4 and 5 end with sections called "Branching Out" that contain some additional activities and recommended readings to expand your experiences.

You will also want to learn more about the Native North American cultures from which the stories come. The map of Native North America at the beginning of this book shows the locations of cultural areas and tribes discussed in the chapters. If you want to learn more about these Native North American cultures, read the descriptions in the "Glossary and Pronunciation Key to Native North American Words, Names and Cultures" at the end of the book.

## Sharing the Stories

These stories are like plants, and you are the gardener. Every time you share a story out loud you bring it to life; you help

*The quiet beauty of winter brings the storytelling season in the Northeast.*

it grow. Many Native North American cultures told stories at specific times of the year. Northeastern peoples told stories indoors during the long cold season between the first and last frosts because the growing season was a time for planting, tending gardens and harvesting. It is said that stories are powerful and that every part of nature stops to listen to a good story. If you plant your crops and the seeds "hear" you tell stories, they might not sprout because they think it is winter, the storytelling season. Your crops could fail. Although you may want to share stories during the growing season, it is good to remember the traditional time and place of storytelling, as well as the Native belief that Earth is alive and listening.

Before you share a story, be sure to look up the meaning of any Native North American words or names in the story that you do not know. These words are defined and explained in the glossary.

Making a storyteller's bag is an easy project. Each object you put into the storytelling bag symbolizes a particular story. Gather things from the natural world or make things to add to the bag. Seeds, feathers, stones, nuts, small carvings—anything that can be jostled around in a bag without breaking can be part of your collection. Read the stories in this book carefully and then use your imagination.

## The Setting of the Story

In many Native North American cultures, everyone was allowed to have a say, and people listened with patience. People would sit in a circle during the time of storytelling because in a circle no person is at the head. All are "the same height." Remembering the circle may help remind you and your listeners that everyone is equal.

Pay close attention to the setting in which you share a story. A quiet place where people can sit comfortably in a circle is best. If other things are going on around you, if some people are sitting outside the group or where they cannot hear well, your story will lose some of its power. Wait until everyone has been brought into the circle before beginning a story.

## Getting Involved in the Story

A good story cannot exist without a good listener. There are certain things that you, as a reader or teller, can do to help your listeners be more effective and more involved. One device is the use of "response words." Tell the listeners that whenever you say "Ho?" they are to respond with "Hey!" That will let you know they are still awake and listening.

If there is singing, chanting, movement or hand-clapping in your story, make sure everyone knows how to do it before the story begins. Then, at the right time in the story, have everyone join in.

One way to make your story-sharing more meaningful is to use Native North American sign language. Many of the signs are the same as those used by the deaf. The widely used sign language that Native North Americans developed is beautiful to watch. Two inexpensive and easy-to-use books that teach Native American sign language through photographs and simple drawings are *Indian Sign Language* by William Tomkins (New York: Dover Publications, 1969) and *Indian Talk: Hand Signals of the North American Indians* by Iron Eyes Cody (Happy Camp, Calif.: Naturegraph Publishers, 1970).

If you are sharing a long story, it sometimes helps to take a short break halfway through. Use this time to have a snack, to share and discuss the story illustrations.

# Going Outdoors

Here are some tips to help you prepare for having safe, fun gardening experiences.

## Preparation

*Prepare thoroughly and well ahead of time.* Plan the activities you want to do and get your supplies ready. Listen to the weather forecast and wear proper clothing for the season, especially on days that are rainy, cold or hot.

## Safety

*Safety* is very important. Choose a garden site where there is no poison ivy, poison oak or poison sumac. *Do not go into areas known for poisonous snakes and other dangerous animals, or where crime is a problem.* Make sure you test for safe lead levels in your soil (see "Testing the Soil" in Chapter 3). High levels of lead are especially dangerous to young children.

Bring along a complete portable first-aid kit. Include anti-bee-sting serum and a snakebite kit and know how to use them. Someone should be certified in first aid as well as CPR for both children and adults.

Include in your outdoor activity kit:

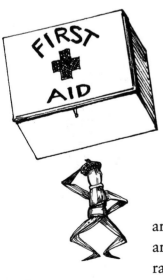

- basic, portable first-aid kit
- clean cloth and an antiseptic liquid with which to clean wounds
- anti-bee-sting serum
- snakebite kit (if you might encounter poisonous snakes in your area)
- small, sharp knife
- insect repellent
- water, especially on hot days
- trash bags

Do not forget to use sunscreen and a sun hat whenever you are working in the sun for more than fifteen minutes. Sunglasses are also a good idea. These will help protect you from the harmful rays of the sun.

## Comfort

*Comfort* is always important. Wear clothes that are appropriate for the weather conditions. A light, waterproof mat or pad is a must so you can sit on the ground in the garden. If necessary, use Earth-friendly insect repellent.

## Fears and the "Yuckies"

*Overcome your fears and prejudices and you will enjoy the natural world.* You may be afraid of a spider, a beetle or something else you find in the garden. If something scares you, do not panic. Slow down, take a deep breath and, if you do not sense any real danger, continue with what you are doing. If you *do* think there is something dangerous at hand, bring it to the attention of an adult. In general, avoid insects and spiders and resist the urge to hurt or kill them. Insects and other small critters are not "yucky," they are just different. Try to appreciate the fact that they are examples of what an incredibly interesting and diverse world we live in.

## Community

*Turn the gardening experience into a way of meeting other people in your neighborhood and the larger community.* Invite neighborhood parents, seniors, older children and community volunteers to help you in the garden and when you are preparing Native meals. Gardens and meals create wonderful places and opportunities for people to gather and build community.

## Conduct

*Go calmly and gently into the garden.* Talking and singing are fun, but *silence* is also very important for getting the most out of your garden experience. *Walk and work softly and in silence* for short periods of time. At these times, talk only when you have a question or when you want to point out something interesting and exciting. When you are being quiet, a bird, insect or small animal may come in very close because it does not know you are there.

*Watch for surprises.* Look closely at your surroundings and you will find a world of exciting events unfolding before your eyes. You might see a hummingbird sipping nectar from squash

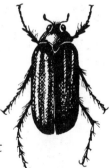

*We can all learn to appreciate that worms, spiders, beetles, slugs (top to bottom) and other creatures all play an important part in the garden ecosystem.*

*This Allen's hummingbird may be feeding its young with regurgitated nectar and insects that it gathered from flowers growing in a nearby garden. Gardens attract many beautiful and fascinating animals.*

flowers. Take the time to marvel at the hummingbird's wings. These experiences are good times for finding out about the amazing relationships between different kinds of plants and animals that live in or visit your garden.

### Nourishment

*Take snack breaks with healthy foods and drinks.* Snack breaks are good times to share special moments. They are also great for sharing one of the stories in this book that relates to the day's activities. Be certain to have on hand lots of cold water and/or natural juices to drink. It is easy to become dehydrated while enjoying your work in the garden on a hot day because long periods of time pass so quickly.

*Leave gum, candy and other foods behind.* Chewing gum and sucking on sweets make it hard for you and everyone else to hear. Sugary, sweet foods dull your taste buds so that the natural sweetness and other flavors of garden foods are overwhelmed. Sugary foods also promote tooth decay. In addition, a simple stick of discarded chewing gum can be deadly to a mole or other small animal that eats it, because the gum forms a block in the animal's digestive system.

## Understanding and Appreciating Other Cultures

You are going to use Native North American stories and activities, and you may be working with people from different cultures in your garden. You will find that people from other cultures look, sound and act different from the people in your family. It is those differences that make it so interesting and exciting to be with people from other cultures!

Always remember to speak to others and act toward them in a respectful way. Be tolerant of things you do not understand and do not make fun of them. Do your best to appreciate cultural differences that can enrich and expand all of our lives. Here are a few simple do's and don'ts that will help you be respectful toward Native North Americans and people from other cultures in general.[1]

- **Don't** "dress like Indians." This is offensive to Native peoples, just as putting on dark makeup for Martin Luther King Day would be to African Americans. Don't make war cries and do other things that mock Native peoples.

Do study and try to understand the special customs of Native peoples and learn from them while keeping your own habits and dress.

- **Don't** refer to Native North Americans with words like "savages," "war-loving" and "primitive." Native cultures are no more backward, warlike or less advanced and civilized than people of other ancestry.
  **Do** talk about the language and customs of local Native people and those from whom the stories come. Try to understand these unique cultures.

- **Don't** say "Let's sit Indian style" or "Let's walk Indian file." Don't call someone else a "squaw" or a "brave." These words offend Native peoples. Many words are misunderstood. Calling someone a "squaw" can be insulting.
  **Do** use simple, direct language like "Let's walk single file," "Let's sit on our bottoms and cross our legs," and refer to others by name or as "boys" and "girls."

- **Don't** speak of Native North American cultures as if they only lived in the past. They have a history *and* are here among us today. Nowadays Native peoples often dress and look much like the other cultures among which they live. They generally do not wear loincloths, headdresses and other Native clothing except during ceremonial occasions.
  **Do** talk about how Native North Americans live in the modern world. They work at jobs, go to school, play sports, drive cars and have family lives much like everyone else. Some live close to the traditional ways and others live a more modern lifestyle. Many Native people are of mixed ancestry; there is no way to tell if someone is Native simply by looking at him or her.

- **Don't** speak as if Native North Americans are from one large culture. Not every Native culture traditionally lived in tepees and hunted buffalo on horseback as certain Plains peoples did in the past. There are more than 550 distinct nations in Native North America, each with its own language, customs, beliefs and ways of living in the world. Many Native cultures have treaties with the larger North American governments, such as the United States and Canada, that recognize their sovereignty and rights as Native nations. **Do** refer to each Native person by his or her tribal name. Discuss the language, beliefs and customs of each culture, honoring its unique people and their connection to the local environment.

*Ella Deal, of the Diné (Navajo) Nation, proudly presents her corn harvest. There are more than 550 distinct cultures Native to North America.*

- **Don't** belittle sacred ceremonies and beliefs by trying to imitate them. It is best to avoid them completely. Ceremonies are the heart and soul of Native cultures and are easily made fun of. They are meant to be practiced by members of a certain culture only. **Do** invite local Native people to visit with you to discuss their beliefs and gardening practices. Study Native ways as a lesson to be understood without being imitated and practiced. Learn more about your own spiritual tradition and how those beliefs support your being close to, and caring for, Earth and other people—for example, Judaism, Islam, Christianity, Hinduism, Buddhism or Baha'ism.

## Using Words That Refer to Native North Americans

In this book, we use the term *Native North American* to refer to Native peoples of the United States, Canada and Middle America. These peoples are often called "Native American" and "American Indian." Not all Native North Americans are

American Indians. The Inuit (Eskimo) peoples of the Far North make up a culture that is distinct from other Native North Americans. Native Hawaiians, also, are usually described as distinct cultures.

In the United States, the terms *American Indian, Native American* and *First People* are all used to refer to the original inhabitants of North America, Central America and South America. In Canada, the terms *Native Indian, Métis, Aboriginal* or *First Nation Member* are commonly used rather than *Native American.* In all cases, it is best to refer first to the person with regard to his or her individual nation, for example, "Zuni," "Tutelo," "Tuscarora" or "Maya."

🐜   🐜   🐜   🐜

This chapter has given you both ideas and directions for using Native North American stories and garden activities. Now it's time to begin!

# The Grasshopper's Song
### (Zuni—Southwest)

Long, long ago there was a grasshopper who had a beautiful corn field. In that garden there was not just corn, but also squash and melon and all kinds of vegetables. All day the grasshopper sat and watched his field and sang.

One day, an old coyote passed by and heard Grasshopper's song. She saw the field filled with all kinds of good food. "What a fine song," she said, "I want to learn that song so I can sing it for my family." So Old Coyote Woman went down into the field and found Grasshopper sitting there.

"Whose field is this?" Old Coyote Woman said.

"It is my garden," said Grasshopper.

"What's that song you are singing?"

"That song is a prayer for the garden to grow well."

"You must teach me that song," Old Coyote Woman said.

"Sit down," said Grasshopper. "I will teach it to you."

Then he taught the song to Old Coyote Woman. "Do not forget it," he said. "You must keep it in your mind until you reach your home. Do not think of anything else."

"I will not forget it," said Old Coyote Woman. Then she started home, holding the song in her mind. But, as she walked along, she saw some doves by the side of the trail.

"Those doves will be good to eat," she said. She tried to sneak up on them, but when she was close they flew away.

"Ah," Old Coyote Woman said, "I have forgotten that song. Grasshopper will have to teach it to me again." So she went back to the grasshopper's field.

"You didn't teach me that song well enough," she said. "You must teach it to me again."

So Grasshopper taught her the song a second time.

Once more, Old Coyote Woman set out for home. This time, as she was going along the trail, a rabbit ran across in front of her. She ran after it, but the rabbit was too fast for her and got away.

"Ah," she said, "I have forgotten that song again." So she went back to Grasshopper. Once again, he taught her the song.

*When harvest time came, they gathered the crops but left some in the field for Grasshopper.*

This time, as soon as Old Coyote Woman left, the grasshopper shook his head. "She will be back again," he said. "But I am not going to teach her the song another time." Then he turned himself into a stone.

Sure enough, just as he expected, back came Old Coyote Woman because she had forgotten the song.

"Teach me that song again," she said. But Grasshopper did not answer her. "I said teach me that song!" But still Grasshopper was silent. "Teach me that song or I will eat you and everything in your field."

But Grasshopper said nothing. Then Old Coyote Woman jumped on him and grabbed him with her teeth to swallow him. But, because Grasshopper had turned himself into stone, her front teeth broke off when she bit him. Old Coyote Woman howled and ran away. Ever since then, all coyotes have had short teeth in front.

Once again, Grasshopper started singing his song. This time a young boy heard him and came down into the field. This boy's mind was clear and good. The grasshopper called to him.

"I am here," Grasshopper called. "Come down into my field."

"Was it your singing that drew me here?" asked the boy.

"Yes," Grasshopper said. "This is my field, and my song is a prayer to make the plants grow. I will give you this field if you will let me live here. But you must save seeds and plant them next year so that I will always have a home."

The boy listened carefully to Grasshopper. "I shall do as you say," said the boy.

Then the boy went home and told his family. They all did as Grasshopper said. They listened to Grasshopper's song and cared for the field. When harvest time came, they gathered the crops but left some in the field for Grasshopper. They saved seeds from each of the plants and planted them the next year. So it was that Grasshopper continued to have a home. So it was that he continued to come each growing season to sing his song.

To this day Grasshopper still sings his song to help the plants grow. You can still find him there in those fields he shared with the people.

Chapter 3

# Gardening for Families

Gardening is a living process—a part of the natural cycle. Each garden is a tiny ecosystem that will succeed if you watch and take your cues from the natural world. Ecological gardening is a simplified form of how nature maintains itself.

Do not worry about being a perfect gardener. Gardening is not complicated and does not require you to be an expert. You can grow as a gardener simply by learning from what you are doing and what you have done in the past.

There are, however, some important things to know before you plan and grow your Native garden. This chapter is an overview of the basic steps that experienced modern gardeners take to prepare and grow an ecological garden that works *with* the cycles of nature. Chapters 1 and 4 immerse you in the important ideas and ways of growing by which you become a part of Native gardening and the Circles of Life. *The basic gardening tips and information in this chapter will help you prepare for planting a specific garden design from Chapter 4—either the Wampanoag or the Hidatsa Three Sisters Garden.*

## Tips for Parents

Children are gardeners at heart. They possess a natural enthusiasm for working with plants. There is little that needs to be done to adapt the day-to-day gardening tasks for children, but it is valuable to consider the approach to take when sharing the activities. Here are a few simple tips:

- Take one step at a time. Explain things clearly and simply and the experience will carry itself.

- Watch for the tasks that each child prefers doing. Encourage children to participate in each of the different gardening experiences to keep their interest, but allow them to do what they most enjoy whenever possible.

- Invite children to take charge of particular crops or parts of the garden to encourage responsible caring.

- Allow a reasonable amount of snacking from the garden and keep a variety of other healthy foods on hand for snack times.

- Allow children to mix short periods of work doing different tasks interspersed with playtime. Gardening is an organic experience that is more effective if children learn that it can also be fun.

- Allow for lots of beginners' mistakes and approach them lightheartedly. Discuss how things could be handled better next time.

- Teach the children that a garden is an attempt to create a temporary natural community or *ecosystem*. Use the garden as a way of teaching about natural cycles, such as the water cycle, nutrient cycle, life cycle, gas cycle, lunar cycle and the cycles of night and day, the seasons and the years. During the gas cycle, for example, people exhale carbon dioxide, which green plants need to grow. Green plants, in turn, give off the life-sustaining oxygen that animals breathe in.

- Use only natural fertilizers and methods of pest control as described in this book. This is important for placing a high priority on the children's health and for teaching wise Earth stewardship.

- Help children to see the garden as a learning laboratory, with lots of opportunities to experiment and observe results.

- Promote the idea that everyone can find their own approach to gardening—there is no one right way.

- Share in the sense of wonder, learning and adventure with the children.

## Keeping a Garden Journal

Schedule quiet time at the end of each gardening day for entries in your *garden journal*. Record the interesting and important things you experienced that day. Be sure to include the date, weather and time of day of your observations. Write down the lessons you learn. This way your knowledge will grow from year to year. Journal entries can also include illustrations and photographs. Try to understand what you are seeing in the garden by asking questions such as who, what, when, where, how and why. What kinds of connections have you noticed between garden plants, animals, soil and so on? Read more about those subjects that interest you. Make copies of the page called "My Garden Journal" and use one page for each day's observations.

# My Garden Journal

Date:_____ Time: _____

**Weather:** general conditions (sunny, cloudy, windy and so on) _____
_____

temperature _____ general wind strength and direction wind is
coming from _____

**What I did in the garden:** _____
_____
_____
_____

**What I saw in the garden:** _____
_____
_____
_____

**Lessons I learned today:** _____
_____
_____
_____

**Illustration or photograph:**

*Garden Journal. Use a separate page to record each day's experiences in the garden.*

# Choosing a Site

*Choose an appropriate site for the garden.* Your site could range from a wide, sloping field near a rural home to a small plot or a rooftop garden in the city. Walk around your land and look at it in a new way. Notice where the sun rises and sets and where the sunlight and shadows fall. Look for a place where the soil is rich. Imagine what your land looked like one hundred years ago, two hundred years ago and beyond. You are about to bring back an ancient way of connecting with nature and seeds in your garden.

Select a site that provides as many of the following things as possible:

- *Plenty of direct sunshine* throughout all or most of the day.

- *A good supply of water.* Plants need, on the average, 1 inch (2.5 centimeters) of rainwater per week during the growing season.

- *A fertile soil of adequate depth.* A rich topsoil of sandy loam that is 1 foot (.3 meter) deep is ideal. Beware of rock outcrops nearby, which indicate a shallow soil. Topsoil can be made deeper and more fertile over time by feeding and enriching the soil using the techniques described in the section of this chapter called "Testing, Preparing and Maintaining the Soil."

- *Well-drained soil.* Water should soak into the soil after it rains—it should not form puddles. Do not plan your garden for a low place where water will pool up. Be certain the top of the water table is well below the surface, even during the wet spring season.

- *A flat slope or one that slopes very gently to the south.* A southwest exposure is best so that the plants will get lots of sunlight during the heat of the day once the dew has evaporated and both soil and plants have warmed.

- *Good air circulation.* Cold air settles into valleys and small depressions. It is better to choose a gentle slope or hilltop.

- *Protection from strong winds.* Mild breezes are healthy, but strong winds can damage crops and erode soil.

- *Plenty of distance from pollutants.* Gardens need to be at least 200 to 300 feet (61 to 91 meters) from the nearest highway because lead (from exhaust fumes), cadmium (from tire wear) and other heavy metals can become part of the growing plant tissues. This makes the plants unfit for eating, especially by children. A 6- to 8-foot (2- to 2.5-meter) evergreen hedge is a good buffer against some highway pollution. Beware of lead from old paint and plaster, sources of asbestos (which also comes from wearing brake linings in vehicles), smokestack emissions from upwind of the site and toxic-waste sites upwind or upstream.

- *Easy, secure access* so that you will not have to carry tools, water and other supplies long distances and so that you will be safe when working in the garden. Locate the site close to human activity if possible to discourage crows, pigeons, raccoons, deer and other plant predators.

- *A manageable size,* large enough to grow your crops but small enough to allow you to grow a satisfying, well-managed garden. Consider how you will water your garden when deciding how big it will be. The specific sizes for the Wampanoag and Hidatsa Three Sisters Gardens are given in the description of the *"Three Sisters Garden"* activity in Chapter 4. It is best if you can use these sizes for your garden, although they can be adapted if your garden space is limited.

- *Soil free of all debris that could hurt you,* such as broken glass, discarded cans and tops, nails, etc.

- A *site free of poisonous plants,* such as poison ivy, oak and sumac.

- A *secure location away from busy traffic and close to the watchful eyes of friendly neighbors* to discourage vandalism.

## Planning and Preparing the Garden Site

Measure the size of your site and plan the entire garden on paper. Later, you will create this garden outdoors. The garden plans offered in this book are included in the *"Three Sisters Garden"* activity in Chapter 4. Whichever garden plan you

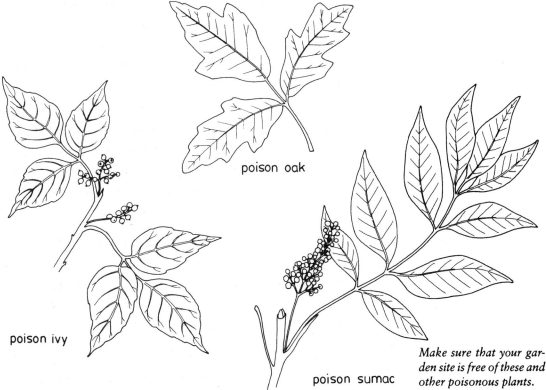

poison oak

poison ivy

poison sumac

*Make sure that your garden site is free of these and other poisonous plants.*

choose, plant the tallest plants on the north side of the garden so they will not cast shade on the shorter plants.

Feel free to plant your own creative garden next to the Three Sisters Garden. We use flowers, herbs and vegetables as an artist uses paints—to create circles, swirls, color combinations and other patterns. As you plan, keep in mind the colors, scents, heights and textures of the plants and their flowers.

Plan a special place in the garden. Once the plants grow, this will be a quiet, sheltered spot where you can spend some time reading, drawing, playing a musical instrument, listening to music or getting involved in some other creative pursuit. We like to have our special spot near the corn or some other tall plants with flowers nearby. Use stones to decorate your spot. Many Native cultures consider stones to be wise because they are the oldest things on Earth.

## Collecting and Caring for Garden Tools and Supplies

Gather the tools and supplies you will need. You can do many things in the garden simply by using your hands. In addition, the basic tools and supplies listed below will allow you to accomplish the garden tasks—from site selection to harvesting—that are described in this chapter. You probably do not need to purchase all of these tools. Start out with a few basic tools and make creative use of whatever you already have at home. Additional supplies you will need are listed in the "Materials" section of each activity.

- work gloves for adults and children
- shovel
- hoe
- metal rake
- spading fork
- three-pronged cultivators
- small trowels for planting and transplanting
- garden cart (best) or wheelbarrow
- hose and nozzle
- watering can
- lawn sprinkler
- compost and/or slow-release organic fertilizer
- tape measure
- ruler

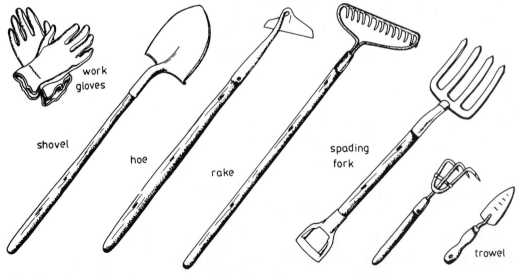

work gloves

shovel

hoe

rake

spading fork

cultivator

trowel

*Some basic garden tools.*

- stakes and strings to help mark the garden rows, corn mounds and so on

- wooden markers or Popsicle® sticks to identify plants

- indelible black marker with a fine enough point to write on wooden markers

- stakes to support plants

- string for tying plants to stakes

- pruning shears

- milk crates or baskets for harvesting

- cooler and crushed ice for harvesting

- containers with lids

- 5-gallon (19-liter) bucket of water and manure

- wide-mouthed jar with lid to measure rainfall (use with ruler)

- bag of cracked corn to put out for raccoons, crows and other pests

You may want to purchase special small tools for children less than eight years old. True Temper makes a line of children's tools called Little Giant. Also, you can obtain a high-quality set of children's garden tools, gloves and other accessories from:

Smith & Hawken
2 Arbor Lane, Box 6900
Florence, KY 41022-6900
(800) 776-3336

Gardener's Supply
128 Intervale Road
Burlington, VT 05401
(800) 876-5520

You can also call the following numbers to request the name of a local dealer of quality children's garden tools from these distributors:

Ames Lawn & Garden Tools
(800) 725-9500

Brio
(800) 433-4363
This company sells gardening tools in specialty toy stores only. Call for the location of stores in your area.

Organize the tool storage area and make sure everyone knows how and where the tools are arranged. Set up a rotating schedule of times at which different people will be responsible for gathering, cleaning and replacing all tools neatly after each gardening session. Each time you garden, it is important to wash dirty tools, wipe them clean and dry them. Clean metal tools with a wire brush every few weeks.

When working, be careful to lay metal rakes and spading forks on the ground with the tines pointing *down*. That way, no one will step on the tines and get hit when the handle flies up. Believe us, it happens!

## Testing, Preparing and Maintaining the Soil

Soil is alive—it is the thin skin of Earth that makes life possible. Plants need soil to grow. Animals eat plants to live. When we feed the soil, we are feeding ourselves and other life on Earth.

*Soil* is made of three basic parts: minerals, organic matter and living things. The *minerals* in the soil are found in sand, silt and clay. *Organic matter* is made up of the dead remains of plants and animals. There are hundreds of different kinds of *living things* in your soil, including earthworms, slugs, mites, nematode worms, beetles, ants and many kinds of insect larvae. (For more information and activities involving soil and the nutrient cycle, see Chapters 8 and 16 of *Keepers of the Earth* [Fulcrum, 1988] and Chapter 6 of both *Keepers of the Animals* [Fulcrum, 1991] and *Keepers of Life* [Fulcrum, 1994].)

Soil is where the *nutrient cycle* takes place. Organic matter is the food for the tiny *soil microbes,* mostly fungi and bacteria, which in turn break down the dead remains of once-living plants and animals into food for living plants. This completes the Circle of Life and Death that makes life possible for both the plants that use sunlight to grow and the animals that eat them.

*Fungi, like these shaggy mane mushrooms, are an important part of the nutrient cycle that enriches the soil, the Circle of Life and Death.*

It is important to have healthy, nutritionally balanced soil in order to grow vigorous plants. Get to know your soil and how to take care of it.

## Testing the Soil

Wait about a month after the snow and ice have melted before you begin to work the soil in your garden. This way the soil will have dried somewhat. It is not good to walk on the soil before it has dried because it will become packed down or *compacted*. You can test the soil. Walk up to the *edge* of the garden, then grab and squeeze a handful of soil into a ball. Push your finger into the middle of the ball; if it crumbles, the soil is ready. If the ball stays whole, wait a bit longer for the soil to dry.

Have a *soil test* done by a local Cooperative Extension Service office. Cooperative Extension Services are usually listed in the phone book under state, county or federal government offices. Shop around for a lab that is not too expensive, and *make sure that the soil test report will tell you the level of lead in your soil.* You may need to look around for a lab that tests for lead.

Do the soil test in the autumn if possible, or in the springtime before you plant after the soil has dried enough to work it. Request a *soil test packet* from the local Cooperative Extension Service. This usually consists of a container and some instructions. Take a few soil samples from the site, mix them together and return them in the container to the Cooperative Extension Service office. You can also buy soil test kits at local garden centers to use for testing pH.

If you cannot locate a local soil testing lab, you may obtain a soil test from the University of Massachusetts Soil Testing Lab. Send a self-addressed stamped envelope and a letter requesting a brochure to the following address:

Soil Testing Lab
West Experiment Station
University of Massachusetts
Amherst, MA 01003
(413) 545-2311

As another alternative, we highly recommend that you contact Woods End Research Laboratory to obtain a soil test. Be sure to call or write about the proper steps to take *before* sending a soil sample.

> Woods End Research Laboratory
> P.O. Box 297
> Mount Vernon, ME 04352
> telephone: (207) 293-2457
> fax: (207) 293-2488

The soil test results will provide information about soil pH, fertility and nutrient needs and any soil preparation that is called for. *Fertile* soil has a good balance of nutrients that helps the plants grow and bear a healthy crop of vegetables. *Organic* nutrients come from leaves, stems and other remains of plants and animals as they decompose. They make up the dark brown part of the soil. *Mineral* nutrients are from the nonliving parts of the soil.

The report will also tell you how much lead is in your soil. Lead is represented by the scientific symbol Pb. If levels of lead are too high, you will end up eating lead in the plants you grow. Lead is particularly hazardous to children. If the lab tells you that the lead level in your soil is unsafe, you will need to find another site to garden. You can avoid problems with lead in the soil by gardening on a site that has never been built upon, is away from major roadways and has never been used for a dump.

### Preparing and Maintaining the Soil

Once the soil is dry enough, loosen it to the depth of a full-sized shovel blade. Start by digging a trench across the width of your garden. Place these shovels of dirt, topside up, into a wheelbarrow. Dig the next trench alongside the first one and place that soil into the first trench. Continue in this way until the whole garden has been tilled, then place the soil from the first trench into the open trench at the end of where you have been tilling. Break the large clods into fine soil. Remove stones, roots and other debris. Wear work gloves in case your soil contains shards of glass, rusty cans or other dangerous objects. Adults may use a rototiller if one is available. Finally, use a metal rake to level the soil and clean away small stones, roots and debris.

Pull up all weeds before you add soil supplements and turn the soil over, or the weeds will keep growing back. Be sure to pull

*Tilling the garden. Store the soil dug from the first trench in the wheelbarrow. Place soil from the second trench into the first trench, and so on across the garden. Finally, use the soil in the wheelbarrow to fill the last trench.*

and dig the roots out when weeding. If you have sown a cover crop, chop up these plants and turn them into the soil. *Cover crops,* which are also called *green manures,* are plants that are grown as a kind of fertilizer and source of organic matter; they add nitrogen to the soil just as adding animal manure does.

If necessary, adjust the pH of your soil by adding limestone, cottonseed meal or sulfur to the garden at the end of the previous growing season, or at least several weeks before actual planting begins. A moderate pH of 6.2 to 6.8 is best. A pH much lower than 6.2 (*acid* or *sour*) means you will need to add some ground limestone. A soil that has a pH greater than 6.8 (*basic* or *sweet*) will need some cottonseed meal or sulfur. Although agricultural sulfur is often used, we prefer to use cottonseed meal to lower pH because it also adds organic matter and nutrients. Spread 5 pounds (2.3 kilograms) of dry cottonseed meal over each 100 square feet (9.3 square meters) of the garden. Sprinkle lime, cottonseed meal or sulfur evenly over the surface of the garden on a calm day, then mix it into the top layer of soil with a metal rake.

If the soil is very low in one or more nutrients, you may need to fertilize to help the crops grow well. This is like adding vitamins to the soil. Always use soil supplements that are the *least soluble,* plus organic. Look for types labeled "colloidal phosphate" for phosphorus, "greensand" for potassium and trace nutrients and "blood meal" for nitrogen.

These nutrients, and the organic matter described below, including well-aged (for six months or more) manure, can be turned into the top layer of soil anytime before planting. If you are using fresh manure, however, it must age before being added to the garden. We like to prepare the soil, add supplements and let the garden sit idle for a week or so before planting. This allows nature to begin working the soil and mellowing it a bit before the seeds and seedlings go in.

Organic matter is extremely important to the soil. It binds the soil grains together, which gives the soil structure and helps it hold moisture. Organic matter also lightens a heavy soil. There are several kinds of organic matter you can feed to the soil. *Compost* is an excellent source of organic matter (see sidebar). *Manure* is also rich in organic matter. Layer a few inches over the garden to add both organic matter and nutrients. We recommend manure from cows, goats or sheep. If this is your first garden, you may find it easier to add peat moss and a blended organic fertilizer in place of the compost, manure and nutrient supplements mentioned above. *Green manures* or *cover crops*, described earlier, are also a great source of organic matter.

## Composting: Baking a Soil Layer Cake

**MATERIALS:** Kitchen organic waste, shredded plant matter (leaves, grass clippings, hay, etc.), ground limestone, manure (aged or fresh), garden soil, shovel, garden cart (preferable) or wheelbarrow, hoe, buckets of water or watering hose.

**DIGGING IN:** Use a compost pile to take part in the nutrient cycle and reduce the tons of organic waste that go into landfills. Homemade compost is an excellent alternative to commercial organic fertilizers.

Start the compost pile in early spring. Locate it in an out-of-the-way spot *downwind* from the house and in a place where runoff from the pile will not flow into a pond, lake, river, stream, ocean, wetland or other aquatic environment. You do not need to build a compost bin. Layer into the pile, from the bottom up:

- **organic matter:** *kitchen waste* (greens, eggshells, coffee grounds, etc., but no meat or cheese scraps because these attract raccoons and other scavengers) and *finely shredded plant matter* (leaves, cornstalks, grass clippings, hay, prunings, etc.)

- **ground limestone**

- **manure** *(aged or fresh)*

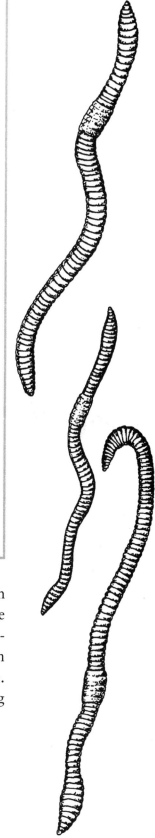

- **soil** (adds a bacterial and fungal culture to the compost pile)

Continue layering these ingredients, from the bottom up, at the following depths and amounts. Repeat these layers as the pile builds:

- 10 to 12 inches (25 to 30 centimeters) of organic matter (kitchen waste and finely shredded plant matter)

- 1 cup (23.7 centiliters) of ground limestone (sprinkled evenly over the top of the pile)

- 2 inches (5 centimeters) of manure

- 1 inch (2.5 centimeters) of soil

Sprinkle a bucket of water over the top of the pile and repeat this once in a while to keep it moist. Be careful not to overload the pile with wastes that are hard to decompose, such as leaves, cornstalks and large, woody material. Feed these in gradually and in small amounts, or chop them up. Do not add bark or wood chips. Concentrate on succulent materials and kitchen wastes. As the compost pile "cooks" it creates a heat of up to 160°F (71.1°C), although the best temperature is around 140°F (60°C). Do not forget to add the soil. The pile will not compost without it!

Continue to build the compost layer cake through the spring, summer and fall. Turn the pile over every few weeks to mix the ingredients well. Begin a new pile when the first one reaches about 4 feet (1.2 meters) high and 6 feet (1.8 meters) across at the base. Your soil layer cake should be done by about midsummer, providing rich fertilizer for garden soil. Allow the compost to cool before putting it in the garden.

Earthworms will naturally migrate to your soil if it is rich in organic matter. You can also add earthworms to the soil (see sidebar). Earthworm droppings, which are called *castings*, improve the fertility of the soil. As earthworms burrow, they loosen up the grains of soil, which helps air and roots to penetrate. Soil that has been worked by earthworms is better at holding moisture.

## Earthworms: Keepers of the Soil

**MATERIALS:** A thousand red worms, compost or aged manure, buckets of water or a watering hose, shovels, garden soil.

**DIGGING IN:** Aristotle called earthworms the "intestines of the Earth." These underground marvels are an important part of the nutrient cycle—the Circle of Life and Death. Earthworms eat soil, leaves and seeds, rotting fruit and roots, manure and tiny creatures such as soil mites and bacteria. They turn this food into fertile droppings called *castings* that contain five times more nitrogen, seven times more phosphorus, eleven times more potassium and 50 percent more bacteria than would be found in soil without worms. Earthworm castings also improve the texture of soil, and their burrows make it easier for air, water and growing roots to penetrate the soil. As if that were not enough, earthworm castings help move acid or basic soils toward a neutral acidity over time.

Fertile, well-balanced soil contains a thriving population of up to two million earthworms per acre (nearly five million earthworms per hectare). Each worm can produce its own weight in fertile castings each day. The best way to increase the number of earthworms in your garden is to maintain a healthy, nutritious soil.

You can also purchase earthworms to add to your soil. One way is to mail-order a thousand red worms. The *Earthworm Buyer's Guide: A Directory of Hatcheries in the U.S.A. and Canada* is available from Shields Publications, P.O. Box 669, Eagle River, WI 54521; (715) 479-4810.

Gather the red worms, tools, compost or aged manure and hose or buckets of water. Dig five holes so that you will spread the worms evenly throughout the garden. Dig each hole to about 1 foot (30.5 centimeters) deep and 1 foot wide. Fill each hole with a 50/50 mix of good soil and compost or aged manure plus two hundred red worms, then water each "worm planting" well. Keep the worm holes moist (not too wet) so that the worms will spread and breed.

## Choosing Seeds

To begin a gardening season, choose the kinds of seeds you want to plant and order them through seed catalogs. You will first need to send a postcard requesting each catalog. (See the *"Native Seeds"* activity in Chapter 4 for a list of addresses to write for seed catalogs.) Native heirloom seeds are recommended for the authenticity of your garden and because planting these seeds helps preserve ancient races of Native crops as

well as biodiversity. (See Chapter 1 and the "Bridges: From Legends to Life" section of Chapter 4 for information on the importance of Native heirloom seeds and biodiversity.) Use organically grown seeds to support Earth-friendly farming and to avoid introducing seeds into your garden that were grown with the aid of chemicals. When choosing seeds, consider:[1]

- eating quality
- days to maturity and time of harvest (the time from planting to when the crop is ready to be picked)
- how strong and hardy the plants are
- appearance
- resistance to pests and diseases
- storage ability
- how well the plants will stand up to frost, heat and drought
- the nutritional value of the crop
- how easy it is to care for, harvest, clean, prepare and preserve the crop. For example, bush beans and non-stake tomatoes will not need stakes or trellises to support them as they grow. Short, stout carrots are easy to harvest, and round onions are easier to prepare than flat onions.
- your interests, tastes and preferences

*Choose seeds of plants that will grow and produce a crop within the length of your growing season.* The length of the *growing season*—the average length of time between the first spring frost and the last autumn frost—varies locally according to slope (north versus south), elevation, location on a hilltop or in a valley and so on. You can determine the number of frost-free days in your area by asking local gardeners and staff at garden centers. In addition, the regional offices of the Cooperative Extension Service and the National Weather Service can provide information on the length of the growing season in your area.

Purchase seeds that give a number for "days to maturity" that fits within the length of your growing season. This information can be found in seed catalogs and on seed packets. Plan to plant your garden after the last spring frost and harvest before the first autumn frost. Allow a couple of extra weeks of growing season to spare in case of late spring frost or early autumn frost.

One way to find out which crops grow well in your area is to ask for advice from your neighbors who garden. Experienced gardeners can also give you planting tips and tell you how to deal with common local pests. Garden clubs and your region's agricultural extension agent are other good sources of information.

Most vegetables, including the Three Sisters crops, are annuals. *Annuals* complete their life cycle in one growing season and have to be replanted each year. *Biennials,* however, require two years to produce their flowers and fruit. *Perennials* live to produce for a number of years and can take more than a year to mature. Many herbs and spices are biennials and perennials.

## Planting, Watering and Growing

Seeds of some plants, such as the squash in the Hidatsa Three Sisters Garden, are best started indoors to produce *seedlings,* especially in colder regions. Many gardeners who live in warmer climates, such as the Southwest, plant squash seeds directly in the garden. Use sterile potting soil and plant two or three seeds in each peat pot about one month before the growing season starts. You will need to plant more seeds than you plan to transplant into the garden, because some will not sprout and others will not grow well. Put seedlings of each variety in trays called *flats* and label them clearly using wooden garden tags or Popsicle® sticks. Water the flats and keep them in a warm, shady place until the seeds sprout, then place them in a sunny location indoors and keep them well watered. A spray bottle works well for watering seedlings. Water the plants deeply every few days for deep root growth. Germinating seeds will die

*Seedlings in peat pots.*

if they dry out. Keep them moist until you see the sprouts.

*Plant by the waxing moon to give strength to your seeds and seedlings.*

Thin the seedlings to one per peat pot when they are a few inches tall. Weed out the weak ones and leave the strong, vigorous plants.

When the seedlings are about 4 inches (10 centimeters) tall and it is warm enough to transplant them, introduce them gradually to the outdoors so that they can adjust. Start by placing the flats outside in a partly shady place for a few hours the first day, a few more hours the second day and so on. Place the flats on a porch, in a tool shed or in some other sheltered place at night. Gradually expose the plants to longer periods of direct sunshine each day.

Some Native American cultures, such as the Tewas of the Rio Grande, plant seeds when the moon is *waxing*—the part of its cycle when it grows larger in the sky. This way the seeds can draw on the strength of the moon to help them grow.

Transplant the seedlings into the garden after about a week of helping them get used to the outdoors. Transplant the hardiest-looking seedlings and compost any that look weak or spindly. Begin by digging holes where each plant is to be placed in the garden. Then, gently peel away about a half inch (1.3 centimeters) from the top of the peat pot. Leave the plant in the peat pot and place it into the hole. (This cannot be done with pots made of other materials.) The top of the soil surrounding the seedling in the pot should be even with the surface of the garden soil. Now press the soil gently but firmly around the seedling and soil. Make a raised ring of soil about 6 inches (15 centimeters) across around each seedling and firm the soil down along the inside edge of the ring. This will help hold water around the roots. Use a watering can to water each seedling *gently* and *deeply* after planting.

When planting seeds directly into the garden, follow the directions given on the seed packets. Pay special attention to the time of planting and how deep you should plant the seeds. Make sure that crops are planted far enough apart to allow space for the plants to grow. Plan for paths of at least 2 feet (50 centimeters) wide between rows of crops. These calculations are great math practice. Be sure to label each row of seeds with gardening tags, as it is surprisingly easy to forget what you have planted where.

*A well-planted seedling ringed by a ridge of soil to hold water close to the roots.*

Plant corn, beans, squash, sunflowers and other larger seeds in individual holes made by poking your finger into the soil. The seeds of some crops, such as carrots and radishes, are planted in furrows dug by running a finger along the soil surface. Cover all seeds with soil and gently pat the soil over them.

Water the entire garden with a gentle, even spray for about an hour after the planting is done. Keep it well watered for the next several weeks as the seeds sprout and the seedlings grow. Keep the garden well watered, but do not overwater. The amount of water a garden needs over time depends on many things, such as the quality of the soil, humidity, air temperature, the kinds of plants and the stage of growth they are in.

When the surface of the soil looks dry, poke a finger down about an inch (2.5 centimeters) into the soil. If the soil is moist just under the surface, there is no need to water. But if the soil is dry down for an inch or 2 (2.5 to 5 centimeters), it is time to water again. It is best to water early in the day. On warm days in temperate climates where water is abundant, you can use a lawn sprinkler and water thoroughly for about an hour to encourage the roots to grow deep. In hot, arid places, such as the Southwest, it is better to irrigate the soil around each plant in order to save water. Irrigation is also better than using a sprinkler on hot days because water droplets can focus the rays of the sun and burn plant leaves.

*Tools for measuring rainfall.*

Another way to find out when the garden needs water is to watch the plants closely. Plant leaves should look green and robust in the morning. It is normal for the leaves of plants to become a bit limp in mid- to late afternoon during the heat of the day. If the soil contains enough water, the leaves will recover their shape overnight. If plant leaves appear wilted in the morning, it is time to water. You should never wait until leaves are so wilted that their edges have begun to turn brown. Any part of a leaf that turns brown has died and will not recover, even after you have watered.

As a general rule, the garden should receive about 1 inch (2.5 centimeters) of water each week. Keep track of rainwater that has fallen by placing a wide-mouth jar on a flat, open space in the garden. Remember to cover the jar on days that it is not raining or when the sprinklers are off so the water does not evaporate. Once a week, use a ruler to measure the depth of the rainwater in the bottom of the jar. If it is less than 1 inch (2.5 centimeters), then water your garden well. The jar should be emptied at least once a week or after you water the garden.[2]

Here are a few helpful tips for growing in the arid Southwest:

- Mulch and lower the planting beds a few inches (5 centimeters) to preserve scarce water. Irrigate to provide a steady supply of water.

- Water early in the day so that plant leaves can dry off. Sudden freezes and high winds can damage wet leaves.

- Create windbreaks such as trees, hedges, walls and overhanging rooflines to shelter the garden.

Be sure to thin the plants within the rows as they grow. Follow the directions on the seed packets or in a gardening book, especially if it was written for your region. A great book with clear, simple directions for growing common garden crops is *The Victory Garden Kids' Book* by Marjorie Waters (Old Saybrook, Conn.: Globe Pequot Press, 1994).

## Weeding

Weed around the young plants once they are several inches high. Be careful not to step on or uproot the seedlings! It will take practice to tell the weeds apart from the crop seedlings. Lay down some mulch of lawn clippings or hay to decrease erosion and moisture loss and to reduce the need for weeding. Our favorite is a thick, 3-inch (8-centimeter) layer of sweet-smelling hay. The hay also makes a nice bed to kneel on while weeding. Weeding is quick work for many hands, and it is a relaxing, centering activity. Large open areas—such as those between mounds in the Native gardens of corn, beans and squash—can be weeded using a weeding hoe, which lightly turns over the soil surface, cuts off small weeds and prevents new ones from growing.

## Eat Your Weedies!

Some plants that are normally called "weeds" can be eaten. The first young sprouts of *dandelion* leaves in the garden make good salad greens. (Older leaves become bitter.) *Lamb's-quarters* or *pigweed (Chenopodium album)* is also edible. The stems and leaves can be boiled like spinach, stir-fried in a bit of butter or eaten raw as salad greens. Pick the leaves and stems when the plant is no more than a foot (30 centimeters) high. *Purslane (Portulaca oleracea)* is an abundant edible garden "weed." The green tips of purslane can be eaten raw in salads, or you can boil the greens for ten minutes and have a tasty, tart pot herb. Purslane can be used to thicken soups, and some people even enjoy pickled purslane. ***Make sure you are absolutely certain about the identification of any plant before you eat it! Plants should be identified by someone who knows them well.***

*Edible garden "weeds" (from left to right): young dandelion leaves, lamb's-quarters (pigweed) and purslane.*

## Feeding the Plants

One way to grow strong, healthy plants with good yields is to feed them some *manure tea* every three weeks or so. Brew up a batch by placing a shovel of well-aged cow manure (about one year old) into a 5-gallon (19-liter) bucket. Now fill the bucket with water. After this has sat for a few hours, scoop up a container of manure tea and feed it to your plants. A beach sand bucket with a handle works well. You can also use an old, long-handled ladle to fill the bucket and pour the manure tea around each plant. When the water of your manure tea no longer gets dark when you stir it, compost the washed-out manure and start over.[3]

## Controlling Pests

Check the plants daily for Mexican bean beetles, corn borers, Japanese beetles and other insect pests. Pick off the insects and put them in soapy water to kill them. Remember that up to one-third of the leaf area of a plant may be eaten without hurting the crop. With healthy soil and companion plants in your Native garden, plant growth will be strong, resistance to insects and diseases will be high and there will be few pests.

cutworm
(actual size of larva =
1 to 2 in. [2.5 to 5 cm])

paper cup collar
around seedling

1 in.
(2.5 cm)

*A simple paper cup collar will protect seedlings from cutworms.*

*Cutworms* like to eat the stems of young seedlings. These pests can be outsmarted by placing a collar around each plant. Simply cut off the bottom of paper cups, slip one cup (upside down) over each seedling and push the lip down about an inch (2.5 centimeters) into the soil.

A piece of reflective aluminum foil that is about 16 inches (40 centimeters) square will help to keep *squash vine borers* away. Place the foil, reflective side up, around the stems of young squash, pumpkin and melon seedlings when they are about 4 inches (10 centimeters) tall. Make a small hole in the center for each stem and cut slits in from the edge to each hole. Slip the foil around the plants, then tape up the slits around each plant. You do not need the cutworm collar if you use this foil mat.

squash vine borer
(actual size of larva =
1 in. [2.5 cm])

cut in foil that's
taped over

16 in.
(40 cm)

*Seedling damage from squash vine borers can be prevented with a shield of aluminum foil.*

Set out some piles of cracked corn away from the garden to attract raccoons, squirrels, chipmunks, deer, crows, pigeons and other animals to keep them from eating crops. If you want to enclose your garden, build a fence using wooden surveyor's stakes or sturdy sticks and chicken wire that is 5 feet (1.5 meters) wide. Dig a trench around the garden and bury about 2 feet (60 centimeters) of the chicken wire in the ground. Since young seedlings can be especially attractive to birds, thorn branches can be used as a temporary barrier to keep them away. The Wampanoag, a woodland people of the East Coast, used to keep crows, grackles and other birds away by having women and older girls sit in small "watcher's-stages" in the garden. From here the watchers would sing, shout and make other noises to scare off the offending birds. Singing drives off bird pests and also helps the crops grow stronger. Scarecrows are used by many Native cultures. Another strategy is to place a mixture of black pepper, red pepper (cayenne) and dry mustard over the planted spots. This sharp-scented blend repels many pesky critters.

Take care to encourage harmless and helpful garden insects, such as ladybird beetles (ladybugs), praying mantids, toads, ants, honeybees and hummingbirds. These critters eat other, harmful species, and some help pollinate the flowers that produce your vegetables.

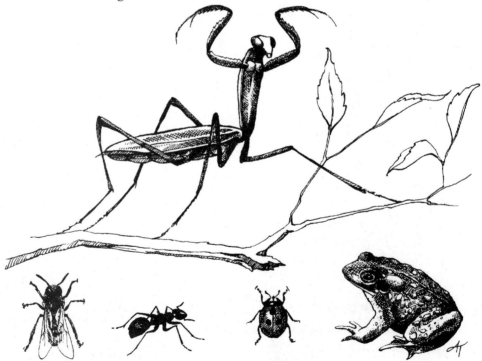

*Some beneficial garden critters (clockwise from the top): praying mantid, toad, ladybird beetle (ladybug), ant and honeybee.*

A *"watcher's stage"* sits at the edge of a traditional Wampanoag garden. As they sat in the watcher's stage, women and older girls sang and made noises to scare away crows, blackbirds and other garden pests.

## Dealing with Vandalism

There are a number of ways to reduce the possibility that your garden will be vandalized or stolen from.

- Educate and involve individuals and groups in your neighborhood who might be inclined to harm your garden. This will help them understand and care about the garden and why it is important. It may even lead them to feel protective of the garden.

- Pick your crops as soon as they are ready to remove temptation, and share them with people who live close to the garden.

- Give your garden a name and put up a sign bearing the name near the entrance. Include an explanation of what your garden is about and how others may become involved if they want to.

- Keep a busy garden! Plan lots of activity around the garden, especially at dusk.

## Harvesting and Preserving

Enjoy the vegetables of your labor! Pick vegetables when they are ripe and put them into a container. Be careful not to pick crops too early or to leave them until over-ripe. A general rule is that, when it looks to be about the right size and color, it is ready to pick. Picking crops on time also encourages the plants to produce more flowers and vegetables.

Gently pull beans off the vine with one hand while holding onto the plant with the other. This will protect the vine from being damaged or uprooted. Pick corn by carefully bending the ears down and twisting. Use pruning shears to cut squash and pumpkins off the vines and leave a piece of stem attached. You can extend shelf life by removing all leaves and other plant parts that are not part of the crop and by cooling the crop immediately in a cooler of crushed ice or other sturdy container kept in the shade. Vegetables, even after harvest, are alive and breathing. Cooling slows the aging process.

Wash all vegetables, dry them and store them in plastic bags in a cool, moist place such as a refrigerator. With a small garden, your eating may keep up with the harvest. Or, you may want to store some of your crops long-term. String beans and snap beans

can be preserved by blanching them in boiling water for about two minutes. Quickly drain the blanched beans and place them in ice water until they cool, then bag them and freeze. Corn can be eaten fresh, blanched and frozen, or dried, removed from the cob and ground into meal for cornbread or Johnnycakes. (See the *"Three Sisters Garden"* activity in Chapter 4 for directions on preparing corn in this way.) Squash stores well in a cool, moist place.

## Putting the Garden to Bed

After the harvest, when the hard frosts arrive, cut off, uproot and compost the stems, stalks and roots. Fall is the best time to test the soil and adjust the pH. You can also feed the soil some organic matter. See the section on "Preparing and Maintaining the Soil" earlier in this chapter for specific tips on caring for the soil when autumn arrives. Once the autumn soil is ready, plant the garden in sweet clover, white Dutch clover or hairy vetch as a green manure, and put a light covering of mulch over the garden to hold the soil in place and enrich it in the spring. Buckwheat, annual rye or oats can also be used. In springtime, before you plant, you will chop up all plant remains and the green manure and turn them into the soil. Be sure to save your garden seeds for planting next spring. See the *"Co-Kokopilau: Keepers of the Seeds"* activity in Chapter 4 for directions on preparing and preserving the seeds for winter storage.

## Rotating the Crops

Keep the garden soil well nourished by rotating the crops from year to year. Each crop affects how the soil develops, as well as its nutrition, texture and the amount of organic matter it contains. Growing the same crop in the same spot year after year uses up certain nutrients in that spot and increases populations of the kinds of pests that eat that crop. Crop rotation helps rebuild soil fertility and control pests. Give your Three Sisters Garden soil a rest by rotating the entire garden to a new spot every few years. This is a traditional practice among many Native North American gardeners. You can alternate your Native garden with another garden in which you grow other favorite crops, such as tomatoes, peas, cabbage, potatoes, carrots, etc. If crop or garden rotation is not possible, soil care and nutrition are all the more important.

## Celebrating the Harvest

Complete the Circle of Celebration. Take time to celebrate and enjoy the vegetables of your labor! Plan a get-together with friends, neighbors and everyone who has helped with the garden. Share some meals, music, dance, games and crafts. Use some of the activities and recipes in Chapters 4 and 5 of this book. You can find many ideas in the *"Native Garden Crafts"* activities (Chapter 4), the *"Cherokee Butterbean Game"* (Chapter 5), in the "Branching Out" sections of those two chapters and in Chapter 5 of *Keepers of the Night* (Fulcrum, 1994).

The ideas and suggestions in this chapter will help you plan, grow and enjoy the fruits of your garden. Chapters 4 and 5 show you how to enjoy and celebrate Native gardens, harvests, meals and crafts. We hope your garden brings you as many fulfilling hours as ours have brought us. Happy growing!

# The Farmer Who Wanted to Be a Jaguar

*(Lacandon Maya—Middle America)*

There was a farmer named Nuxi who had a fine milpa. In his garden many things grew. Corn and beans and squash and tomatoes grew there. There were banana trees, oranges and grapefruits, guavas and passionfruit, pomegranate and sapodilla. There was manioc and sweet potatoes.

However, though Nuxi's milpa was in a part of the rainforest close to his house, the animals began to raid that garden during the night. The coatis and the howler monkeys, the agoutis and the deer and other animals would come each night. Each night they would come and take guava and bananas and fruits from the trees. They would eat corn and beans from his garden.

Whenever Nuxi went to his garden and discovered that some of his crops had been taken by the animals he would grow angry. He tried waiting in his milpa to drive the animals away. But, because he worked in the garden during the day, he could not stay awake all night. And when he slept the animals would come and steal his crops.

Finally, Nuxi became so angry he could stand it no longer. He began to burn copal incense and he prayed to Akinchob, the patron of farmers.

"Hear me," Nuxi prayed, "I want to be turned into a fierce jaguar. Then I will be able to stay awake all night. Then I will be able to guard my milpa and keep out all of those useless animals."

As he burned incense and prayed, the smoke rose. Akinchob, the patron of the milpa farmers, smelled the good scent of copal and came to listen. He listened to Nuxi's prayer.

"He has done his offering properly," Akinchob said. "If that is his wish, that is what I will give him."

Then, shaking his head over the foolishness of some men, Akinchob turned Nuxi into a jaguar.

As soon as Nuxi became a jaguar, he was very pleased. He was large and powerful. His eyes were keen enough to see in the dark. His voice was loud and deep and frightening. His teeth and claws were long and sharp.

"*Neh tsoi*," Nuxi Balam growled, "This is very good. Now no useless animals will dare to enter my milpa." He began to

*"You people," he growled, "come inside and help yourselves to my crops."*

walk around the outside of his farm, watching for any who might try to come inside.

But, as Nuxi Balam walked around his milpa, he began to notice people in the forest around it. Those people looked hungry and he took pity on them.

"You people," he growled, "come inside and help yourselves to my crops. I am guarding this milpa from those useless animals, but I am always ready to share with my own people."

Then the people of the forest came inside and began to eat.

From that day on, the people of Nuxi's village no longer came to the part of the forest where the jaguar farmer had his milpa. For, now that he was an animal, people looked like animals to Nuxi Balam. And those hungry people of the forest he invited in to share his crops were the same animals he had once tried so hard to chase away.

# Chapter 4

# Traditional Native Gardening

## The Bean Woman
### (Tutelo—Southeast)

Long ago, the animal people and the plant people lived together in a village beside the river. One morning, just as the sun was rising, all the men of that village heard the sound of a woman's voice singing downstream from the village. It was Bean Woman and this is what she sang:

> Who will marry me?
> Who will marry me?
> Let him ask if he
> wants to marry me.

Her voice was very beautiful. Many of the men in the village followed the sound of her voice to the place where Bean Woman sat by the river singing. The first to reach her, for he was a very fast runner, was Mountain Lion Man.

"I will marry you," Mountain Lion Man said. "Will you accept me as your husband?"

Bean Woman stopped singing and looked at Mountain Lion Man who crouched there in front of her, swinging his long tail from side to side.

"If I marry you," she said, "what food will I have from you to eat?"

"I am a great hunter. You will always have plenty of meat," Mountain Lion Man said.

"Then if I married you I would die for I never eat that kind of food," Bean Woman answered.

So Mountain Lion Man went away.

The next to arrive was Deer Man.

"I will marry you," Deer Man said, "if you will accept me as your husband."

Again Bean Woman stopped singing. She looked at Deer Man, who stood there stomping his feet, his broad antlers

*Then Bean Woman rushed forward and threw her arms around Corn Man's neck.*

raised high. "What food will you give me to eat?" Bean Woman said.

"I will give you the tender bark of trees and sweet buds," Deer Man said. "That is what I eat and what you would eat as my wife."

"Then I cannot marry you," Bean Woman said. "I have never eaten such food and I would die."

Deer Man went sadly away. As soon as he left, Bean Woman began again to sing her song.

> Who will marry me?
> Who will marry me?
> Let him ask if he
> wants to marry me.

Before long, Bear Man came out of the forest. He came up to Bean Woman and she stopped singing.

"I will marry you if you accept me," Bear Man said.

"What kind of food will you give me to eat?" Bean Woman asked, looking up at Bear Man as he stood there swaying back and forth on his hind legs.

"The best food of all," Bear Man said. "I will give you all kinds of nuts and berries and grubs and honey."

"Then I would die if I married you," Bean Woman said. "I cannot eat that kind of food."

So Bear Man, too, went away and Bean Woman continued her song.

> Who will marry me?
> Who will marry me?
> Let him come and ask if he
> wants to marry me.

But as she was singing, she sensed the presence of someone who had appeared as quietly as if he had come up out of the moist earth. She stopped singing and looked up. Corn Man stood there close beside her, tall and straight, his golden hair blowing in the wind.

"I will marry you if you will accept me," Corn Man said in a soft voice.

"What food will you give me as your wife?" she said.

"Only sweet corn," Corn Man said. "I will give you that and no other food."

"If that is so, I will gladly marry you."

"It is so," Corn Man said, opening his arms. "Come to me and be my wife."

Then Bean Woman rushed forward and threw her arms around Corn Man's neck.

"This is how it was meant to be," Bean Woman said as she embraced Corn Man. "The Great Creator made us to always be with each other."

So it is that to this day, whenever you walk into the fields which are planted in the old Tutelo way, you will see the bean plants twined around the corn in a loving embrace.

🐞　🐞　🐞　🐞

## Bridges: From Legends to Life

When Corn Man appears to Bean Woman in the Tutelo story "The Bean Woman," she knows instantly that she has found her husband-to-be. Neither Mountain Lion Man, Deer Man nor Bear Man is right for her. Some things complement one another and some do not. To this day in traditional Native Tutelo gardens and those found throughout North America, Bean Woman still wraps her arms around Corn Man as they grow together.

Gardening is a cooperative activity. Every gardener needs to work together with others, and this can happen only if we listen well to each other. In the Zuni story of "The Grasshopper's Song" that appears earlier in the book, Coyote has good intentions but does not listen to Grasshopper's directions. Coyote keeps forgetting the song that Grasshopper is trying to teach her. Coyote shows us the importance of listening well.

The boy, however, *hears* what Grasshopper has to say. At harvest time, he and his family leave some of the crop for Grasshopper. They also save the seeds and plant them the next year so that Grasshopper will continue to have a home. This family realizes that, in order to receive from the garden, we must give something back. This is how each of us can be part of the Circle of Giving and Receiving.

It is a tradition among many Native North American gardeners to plant extra measures of each crop. This way there will still be enough to feed the people after the grasshoppers and other insects, raccoons, rabbits and other animals have had something to eat. Planting extra food reminds us that other animals are important and that they, too, must eat. Being generous is simple, practical wisdom that enables the people to harvest what they need to survive.

Everyone was provided for in traditional Native communities.

*Plant more crops than you need so there will be enough to share with the wild creatures who visit your garden, such as this mule deer fawn.*

When food was scarce, people simply shared what was available. Nowadays, in some areas there is a renewed sense of this kind of generosity. Many programs provide fresh produce to homeless or low-income people who have no money and lack the skills or garden space to grow their own food. These programs are usually run by local food banks.

### Native North American Gardening: Past and Present

Close to East St. Louis in southern Illinois, near where the Missouri River empties into the Mississippi, there once was a city of twenty thousand people. This was the largest ancient city in America north of Mexico. The building of this great city and its 120 original earthen pyramids began around fourteen hundred years ago, before the coming of the Roman Empire, and it lived on through Europe's Renaissance.[1] The Cahokia Mounds, as they are now known, are among the greatest earthwork pyramids ever created. One of these mounds, called "Monk's Mound," has a greater volume and overall size than Egypt's largest stone pyramid of Khufu (Cheops).

Not far from Monk's Mound stood a gigantic circle 410 feet (125 meters) across that was made of massive wooden poles. The largest pole stood in the center. This circle, which was built about a thousand years ago, was a giant solar calendar that was used for gardening. It kept track of the seasons and the movement of the sun.[2]

Today the ruins of the Cahokia Mounds remind us that great cities could be built where crops were grown and food was plentiful. Cahokia was built at about the same time that the hoe and new kinds of *maize* (corn) were brought to this region from Mexico in the tenth century.[3]

The Incas, Maya and Aztecs were the first to grow corn, beans and many of today's food crops. Maize became the staple food for the Hohokam and other peoples of the arid Southwest. Ranging from Argentina and northern Chile to southern Canada, varieties of maize were bred that grew well in every environment.[4]

In the past, Native North Americans in Canada and Alaska lived by *foraging*—hunting, gathering and fishing. In addition to foraging, the Native people of Middle America, where there were great cities, grew a variety of crops. In between these northern and southern peoples were many cultures that both foraged and farmed.

MIDDLE AMERICA. Maize was first grown by Native peoples around seven thousand years ago, who adapted it from a wild grass called *Teosinte*. This grass still grows in the wilds of southern Mexico, Honduras and Guatemala. The Maya were one of the first peoples to breed corn, which made up 80 percent of their ancient diet. Corn was often prepared by the Maya as a kind of flatbread called a *tortilla* (tor-tee´-uh).

Mayan civilization used many kinds of agriculture to grow the food that fed their great cities. *Raised fields* were created in low-lying wetlands that were drained with ditches. *Terraced gardens* were built into steep hillsides using stone retaining walls to prevent erosion. Corn, beans, squash, gourds, chiles and cotton were among the crops grown in these gardens. Many root crops and both fruit and nut trees were planted near the houses in *yard gardens* or *kitchen gardens,* especially the ramón nut or breadfruit tree. Among other tree crops used for both food and shade were:[5]

### Teosinte

*Teosinte, a wild grass, is among the most ancient ancestors of today's corn. Teosinte comes from a Nahua (Aztec) word meaning "mother of corn" (shown life-size).*

- avocado
- cacao
- papaya
- guava

- allspice
- nance
- calabash
- hogplum

- mamey zapote
- coyal palm
- copal
- sapodilla

The traditional Maya have also used *milpa* or *swidden* farming for about four thousand years. First, an area that has rich, well-drained soil is cut and burned to make a clearing. Trees and root crops are planted to hold the soil in place and keep nutrients from being lost. Over the years, milpa farmers have planted maize, beans and some eighty other crops. Milpa farming uses many gardening techniques, including crop rotation, weeding, layering, companion planting, mulching and fertilizing.[6] Each acre grows as much as 2.7 tons (2.4 metric tons) of shelled corn per year.[7] After three to seven years of gardening, the soil tires and the old plot is left *fallow* (unplanted) for anywhere from four to twenty years, depending on the climate, the kind of soil and how quickly it can replenish itself. Because they use young forest lands over and over again for agriculture, the traditional Maya are able to preserve large, untouched stands of mature rainforest.

*The Anasazi, who built these magnificent cliff dwellings at Mesa Verde, were expert desert farmers. The "Cliff Palace" ruin shown here contains 217 rooms.*

By hunting and collecting wild plants from the surrounding forest, the Maya round out their existence. The trees, such as rubber, cacao, citrus and balsam, which are planted in the old milpa plots, provide food and shelter for many animals that are part of the Mayan diet.

SOUTHWEST. The kind of traditional gardens grown by Native North Americans depends on the amount of rainfall, length of growing season, amount of sunshine and kind of soil found where they live. In much of the windy, arid Southwest, water is scarce for much of the year, there is plenty of sunshine and there is little of the brown *humus* (hyou´-mus) in the soil that makes it rich and fertile. At high elevations the days are warm and nights are very cool. In this land of the Hopi, Apache, Diné (Navajo) and other cultures, crops must be planted in the springtime after the soil has thawed but while there is still enough moisture for the seeds to sprout. Once the warm weather comes, the soil dries out quickly. Some cultures, such as the *Akimel O'odham* or "River People," who are also known as the *Pima*, irrigate their crops with water.

Traditional southwestern cultures grew corn, beans and both summer and winter squash. Southwestern varieties of corn and beans created a rainbow of colors. Corn was a staple crop for many peoples, including the Hopi, Tewa, Zuni and *Tohono O'odham* or "People of the Desert," the *Papago*. The Hopi alone grew twenty varieties of corn. Two important kinds of beans were the tepary bean and the pinto bean, which is really a variety of the kidney bean. Tepary beans, especially, can tolerate the hot, dry southwestern climate. Beans were important to many cultures, such as the O'odham, Zuni and Quechan (Yuman). Pumpkins and other kinds of squash were commonly grown by the Apache, Diné and Havasupai, among other southwestern peoples.

PLAINS. The traditional peoples of the Plains live in a semiarid land with ribbons of forest growing along the riverbanks. People in a traditional plains village, such as the Mandan, Hidatsa, Arikara and Atsina (Gros Ventre), grew corn, beans, squash, sunflowers and tobacco in the bottomlands along the rivers. Garden plots were rotated and left fallow for a few years when the soil became depleted. These cultures also fished, gathered mussels and hunted waterfowl. They hunted small animals in valley forests and bison on the upland plains. Cultures who live in the lower Colorado River region traditionally plant corn two times each year: in February when the trees begin to bud, and again in August.

Although many people today picture Plains people as horseback riders who hunted bison while roaming the plains, this was only true for a brief period in the history of certain cultures. The Cheyenne, for instance, left farming in the late eighteenth century when they were introduced to horses and took up a nomadic life as bison hunters. When the great bison herds were wiped out in the late nineteenth century,[8] the Cheyenne returned to farming and became expert horse breeders.

EASTERN WOODLANDS AND SOUTHEAST. Farming is a strong tradition throughout the East, ranging from the Southeast to around the Great Lakes and east through what is now called northern New England and the Maritime Provinces. Water is abundant in many areas. Traditional gardens were planted with corn, beans and squash, among other crops. Sunflowers were grown by some southeastern peoples, such as the *Aniyunwiya,* the "Real People" (Cherokee). Each family among the Cherokee had its own garden plot, but most of the food was produced in large communal gardens in the fertile river valleys.

Many cultures moved their gardens and villages at certain times to allow the fields to lie fallow so the soil could replenish itself.[9] The Huron and Haudenosaunee (Iroquois) moved every eight to ten years. Abenaki fields along the Connecticut River and Wampanoag fields on Cape Cod were also allowed to lie fallow. Among the Narragansetts, every two years of farming was followed by a fallow year.

We may never know for certain whether or not the story of Squanto showing the Pilgrims how to fertilize their soil with fish is accurate. Evidence shows that certain Native peoples in southern New England used fertilizer, but only in poor or worn-out soil. Some Native people, for example, prepared the soil ahead of time by placing two or three alewives (herrings) in the spots where seed was to be planted or, if there was no chance to prepare the soil beforehand, next to where the plants were growing.[10] Fish do not make a good fertilizer, however, and this practice is not recommended.

## Traditional Three Sisters Gardens

Successful gardeners know that everything must be done at the right time of year. Traditional Native North American gardeners keep a close watch on the seasons and the crops. They hold many garden celebrations. The coming and going of the moons are reminders of the seasons for planting, hoeing and harvesting.[11]

THE THREE SISTERS. Corn, beans and squash—the *Three Sisters*—are grown from the Northeast to the Southeast, from the Plains to the Southwest and into Middle America. Although many Native North American cultures grow corn, beans and squash, the tradition of calling these crops the "Three Sisters" originated with the Haudenosaunee, the "People of the Longhouse," who are also known as the Iroquois.

In late spring we plant the corn and beans and squash. They're not just plants—we call them the Three Sisters. We plant them together, three kinds of seeds in one hole. They want to be together with each other, just as we Indians want to be together with each other. So long as the Three Sisters are with us we know we will never starve. The Creator sends them to us each year. We celebrate them now. We thank Him for the gift He gives us today and every day.[12]

—Chief Louis Farmer
*Onondaga*

Many kinds of Three Sisters Gardens are grown throughout Native North America. The *"Three Sisters Garden"* activity shows how to create two forms of Three Sisters gardening—those of the Wampanoag people in the Eastern Woodlands and the Hidatsa of the Plains.

The traditional Three Sisters Garden forms a community of plants and animals—an *ecosystem*—that lasts for the growing season. It does not use plowing and relies on the natural relationships between corn, beans and squash. These three crops help each other grow in the Native garden—they are a form of *companion planting*.

Beans are a *legume*—a member of the pea family. Legumes have certain bacteria that live in nodules on their roots. These bacteria absorb nitrogen from the air and change it into the *nitrates* that plants need to grow. This is called *nitrogen fixation*. In this way, beans fertilize the soil for the corn and squash plants. As in the story "The Bean Woman," beans get the support they need to grow by winding around the cornstalks. Squash plants grow as a ground cover between the corn and beans. The large squash leaves lessen erosion, prevent weeds from growing and increase the amount of rain that soaks into the soil.

Three Sisters gardening creates a fertile soil in which strong plants grow that resist damage from diseases and insects that would normally consume and even destroy them. The corn, beans and squash even attract beneficial insects that prey on those that are destructive.[13] Most Three Sisters fields are planted using small

*Bean vines climb cornstalks and insects feed in the community of the Native Garden.*

mounds. Unlike planting rows, which channel rainwater and can cause soil erosion, mounds slow the flow of water and help hold the soil in place.

Most modern farms use *monoculture*—a large area is used to grow just one kind of crop. When different kinds of crops are grown together in the traditional Three Sisters Garden, it is called *polyculture,* and corn yields are up to 50 percent higher.

Traditionally, many Native North Americans plant extra amounts of each crop to feed the insects and other animals that invade the garden. They also feed crows, raccoons and other creatures by putting out small piles of seed, such as cracked corn, away from the garden for the animals to eat instead of the crops. Scarecrows are used by the Zuni, Hidatsa and many other cultures. Some Native people use fences to keep out pests. In certain cultures, such as the Wampanoag, small shelters raised on platforms are built in the garden. Women and older girls who sit in these shelters sing and make noise to scare the birds away. The Hidatsa children who sit in a *watcher's stage* drive the crows, magpies and other pests away by singing to let their presence be known. Hidatsa farmers also believe that singing helps the crops grow stronger.

## Native Crops

Generations of Native gardeners from North, Central and South America have saved and grown the seeds of many different wild and domesticated crops. These foods have forever changed the world. Here is a list of just a few crops that are the gifts of the Native Americans: sassafras, tomato, potato, squash, maize (corn), pumpkin, bean, cotton, maple syrup, cranberry, chili, garlic, tobacco, peanut, pecan, blueberry, strawberry, avocado, vanilla, allspice, chocolate, wild rice, Jerusalem artichoke, sweet potato, butternut, chestnut, hazelnut, beechnut, black walnut and hickory nut (staples of the Muskogee and other peoples of the Southeast), cassava (manioc), sunflower seed, red and green pepper, prickly pear, gourd, goosefoot, amaranth, wintergreen and some varieties of mint. Native Americans have also given the world many berries, spices, flavorings, nuts and other useful plants.

## Native Seeds and Garden Cycles

*Soil* is necessary for the nutrient cycle, which is part of the Circle of Life and Death on Earth. Earth is where living things go when they die, and where life springs anew every time a seed sprouts. Many of today's seeds are here because of the work of countless generations of Native gardeners. These are the seeds of plants that have been bred because they have the most desirable taste, color, nutrition and the ability to adapt to particular soils, climates and planting patterns.

Native gardeners have always found it important to store seeds for the next growing season. Mayan peoples stored corn in underground grain stores called *chultuns*. The Pawnee and Hidatsa peoples stored their food and seed in grass-lined pits. Some eastern peoples used to line storage pits with bark. Many cultures of the dry Southwest stored seeds in aboveground containers.

Native communities of the early 1600s, such as the Wampanoag and Massachusett, taught the newly arrived Europeans how to *plant* seeds individually rather than *sowing* seeds by tossing them on the ground, as was the custom in Europe. Over the course of many generations, by carefully selecting and planting seeds from preferred plants, Native Americans have chosen certain varieties of plants for their gardens. Native gardeners have also created *hybrids* by making sure that pollen from the flowers of one desirable plant fertilized the flowers of another chosen plant. The new hybrid shared the desirable

*Ears and silks are the female parts of the corn plant (bottom). Each silk forms a single kernel of corn on that ear when fertilized with pollen from the male flower or tassel (top).*

qualities of both parent plants. Hybridization was sometimes done by actually transferring the pollen from flower to flower or by planting certain species close together so that they cross-pollinated naturally.[14,15] In these ways, many varieties of Native corn were developed that had colors of red, yellow, blue or purple, could grow in arid deserts of the Southwest or in wet areas, thrived in the mountains or coastal plains and could bear a crop after growing for only sixty days to as long as three months or more. Corn was bred with a husk to shield against disease, insect pests and bad weather. The Tohono O'odham people developed a corn that grows close to the ground and conserves water by having a small amount of leaf and stalk. New varieties of Native plants are constantly being discovered.

Plants bred and saved for local conditions are known as *heirloom seeds, folk varieties, crop ecotypes* and *land races*. Heirloom varieties preserve the genetic "memory" of all the generations of seeds that came before them. The Cherokee people still plant varieties of corn that are found only in eastern North America. Maize seeds in the moist eastern woodlands are usually planted about 1 to 3 inches (2.5 to 7.6 centimeters) deep, but Hopi and Navajo farmers of the dry Southwest bred corn seeds that can be planted 8 to 12 inches (20 to 30 centimeters) deep in sand where the soil stays moist.[16] This dryland corn must be able to do something that eastern corn cannot: it must grow up through a lot of topsoil to reach the surface.

*Varieties of Native crops: corn, beans and chilies. Scotch Bonnet chilies are in the basket.*

**SOWING SEEDS OF THE FUTURE.** Many kinds of wild plants, as well as the Native garden seeds and crops that were bred from them, are disappearing. We must find and preserve the remaining Native wild plants and garden varieties as well as the habitats they need to survive. It is important to preserve a

high *diversity*—many different kinds—of wild and garden varieties in order to make sure that future generations of plants and people have choices to help them survive. Every plant has unique qualities of pest resistance, drought tolerance, adaptability to various soils, tolerance to heat and cold, nutritional and medicinal uses and flavors. Plants with a higher diversity are better able to adapt to and survive changes and extremes in the environment. For instance, individuals of a certain kind of plant that can tolerate a drought will live through a dry period and keep the species going. Plants with only a few individuals left have a much smaller chance of adapting and surviving.

All gardeners should be encouraged to grow Native varieties. Three groups that are doing the important work of growing and preserving Native crops and seeds are the Seed Saver's Exchange on Heritage Farm in Decorah, Iowa; Native Seeds/SEARCH in Tucson, Arizona; and the Seeds of Change Farm in Santa Fe, New Mexico.

## Seeds of Change

Some favorite corn varieties available from the Seeds of Change catalog are the Rainbow Inca, Black Aztec and Hopi Pink. Mandan Red corn has a 2-foot (61-centimeter) deep taproot that helps support the plant and absorbs moisture from deep in the soil. This variety of corn grows well at high, dryer elevations. The tepary bean, which is native to the southwestern Sonoran region, is drought tolerant, high in protein, resistant to bean beetles and has a pleasant, nutty taste. Scarlet runner beans, which produce striking scarlet flowers, are a favorite among many Native cultures in the Southwest and Mexico. These beans are great climbers and work well in a Three Sisters Garden. Scarlet runners produce mottled, purple and black "jewelry beans" up to 1 inch (2.5 centimeters) long, which are strung by children into necklaces.

By using Native seeds, we become part of the Circle of the Generations in Native agriculture. Each of us can be like the Kokopilau, the Hump-Backed Flute Player of Hopi tradition.[17] Kokopilau brings good fortune, fertility, music and culture. He travels around the world carrying the seeds of corn, beans, squash and flowers in his hump. As Kokopilau travels and plays his flute, the lands and the winds become warm, the rains come, and he spreads the seeds of these good plants.

Native seeds and gardens link us to the rich tradition of caring for the plants that humans depend on for survival. With every planting we help to keep a species alive; we play our part in the Circle of Life. Gardening is an act of healing, an affirmation of life and a show of faith and hope for the future of this generation and those to come.

## Activities

### Native Seeds: Holding the Future in Your Hands

**ACTIVITY:** Collect, discuss and enjoy observing and learning about seeds of your favorite Native North American crops as well as those you plan to plant in your Three Sisters Garden. Use seeds to create your own original designs.

**MATERIALS:** Seeds of Native crops, seed catalogs, paper, pencils, crayons, white nontoxic glue, posterboard

*Kokopilau, the Hump-Backed Flute Player.*

**DIGGING IN:**

1. Brainstorm a list of crops you believe are gifts of Native North Americans. Check this list against the list of Native crops mentioned in the "Bridges: From Legends to Life" section of this chapter and in the Introduction (Chapter 1). Why did you choose the crops you did? How many of them are really native to the Americas? Are you surprised by your findings? Add to your list of Native crops from those given in this book.

2. Draw or write down your four favorites from this list of Native crops. Have everyone you are working with do the same. Tally up the lists to reveal the dozen or so most popular crops.

3. Coordinate this part of the activity with choosing crops and ordering seeds for the Three Sisters Garden you plan to grow (see the next activity). If you decide to do this, make sure that the seeds you obtain include several Native varieties of corn, beans, squash and sunflower. Be careful to order seeds for a few varieties of the kinds of beans that are eaten fresh, such as string, green, snap and wax beans. Also make sure you get some seeds to grow beans that you will dry and store, such as kidney, lima, black, common and tepary beans.

You may also want to purchase gourd seeds. See the *"Growing, Drying and Finishing Gourds"* activity later in this chapter for more details about the kinds of gourd seeds to look for and where to get them.

**4.** Obtain the seeds for varieties of these crops that are suited to your local climate and growing season. Find out the length of growing season in your area by following the directions given under the section called "Choosing Seeds" in Chapter 3. Make sure that the seeds you order and/or purchase will mature within the length of your growing season.

Seeds may be purchased at a local nursery, through heirloom seed catalogs, from a seed saver's exchange or from a source of traditional Native American crops. Following are a few highly recommended Native seed sources.

*A variety of Native seeds in storage at the Native Seeds/SEARCH Farm.*

**Native North American Seed Varieties:**

Seeds of Change
P.O. Box 15700
Santa Fe, NM 87506-5700
(505) 438-8080

Seeds of Change has educational resources as well as films and information about upcoming conferences.

Native Seeds/SEARCH
2509 North Campbell Avenue
Suite 325
Tucson, AZ 85719-3304
(520) 327-9123

This organization also has VHS tapes, slides and curriculum materials that teach about the work of finding and preserving Native seeds in the Southwest, as well as their work using Native crops of the Southwest to control diabetes.

Eastern Native Seed Conservancy
P.O. Box 451
Great Barrington, MA 01230
(413) 229-8316

This organization preserves, propagates and distributes both Native and non-Native heirloom varieties, with an emphasis on the seeds of eastern and northern plants. In addition to distributing seeds to eastern Native peoples, the Eastern Native Seed Conservancy has established a general seed-saver's network called the Conservation and Regional Exchange by Seed Savers (CRESS).

**Heirloom Seeds:**

Abundant Life Seed Foundation
P.O. Box 772
Port Townsend, WA 98368
(206) 385-7192

Bountiful Gardens
c/o Ecology Action
5798 Ridgewood Road
Willits, CA 95490
(707) 459-0150

Garden City Seeds
1324 Red Crow Road
Victor, MT 59875
(406) 961-4837

Johnny's Selected Seeds
Foss Hill Road
Albion, ME 04910
(207) 437-9294

(Johnny's specializes in short-season/cold-climate varieties.)

Seeds Blüm
HC 33
Idaho City Stage
Boise, ID 83706
(208) 342-0858

Southern Exposure Seed Exchange
P.O. Box 170
Earlysville, VA 22936
(804) 973-4703

Seed Saver's Exchange
3076 North Winn Road
Decorah, IA 52101
(319) 382-5990

The members of Seed Saver's Exchange plant and preserve more than five thousand varieties of heirloom seedstocks.

5. When the seeds arrive, pass them around for all to observe. Use a pencil to draw a design on a piece of posterboard. This design could be a flower, a vegetable or simply a beautiful pattern. Plan to use some of your colorful seeds like paint pigment to create your own original work of art. Each color will be made up of a number of seeds from a particular garden plant. Glue and label some of the seeds from each crop onto the posterboard to create your art. Label each kind of seed and use this art as a reference chart.

## Three Sisters Garden: Corn, Beans and Squash

**ACTIVITY:** Plan, plant, nurture, harvest and enjoy a traditional Native North American garden of corn, beans and squash, the "Three Sisters."

**MATERIALS:** The basic gardening tools and supplies you will need are listed under "Collecting and Caring for Garden Tools and Supplies" in Chapter 3. In addition, you will need seeds for several Native varieties of corn, beans, squash and sunflower that are adapted to local climatic conditions, including length of growing season. (Gourd seeds are optional.) Find the length of the growing season in your area by taking the steps suggested under the section called "Choosing Seeds" in Chapter 3. Make sure that the seeds you order from the catalogs listed in the *"Native Seeds"* activity will have enough warm weather to mature where you live. Both of these Three Sisters Gardens traditionally use a variety of flint corn. If you live in a very cold or very hot climate, you may need to use varieties different from those in the descriptions for the Wampanoag

*Desert varieties of the Three Sisters: corn, beans and squash.*

and Hidatsa Three Sisters Gardens.

You will also need: several small sticks to mark the locations of mounds (the number will depend on the size of your garden and the number of mounds it will hold), paper, pencil, tape measure, yardstick or meter stick, cracked corn and compass.

For the Hidatsa Three Sisters Garden you will need these special supplies to sprout the squash seedlings: peat pots, potting soil, seedling flats, spray bottle and watering can.

**DIGGING IN:**

1. Before proceeding with this activity, read Chapter 3 and carefully complete the tasks that are necessary to begin your garden. Continue to refer to Chapter 3 as you grow, care for, harvest and complete your garden.

2. Pay close attention to planning the shape and size of your garden. We offer two versions each of both the Wampanoag and the Hidatsa Three Sisters Gardens: a square and a round form. The square gardens measure 20 feet (6 meters) along each edge and have a surface area of 400 square feet (37 square meters). You can also create a round garden to symbolize the Circles of Life. The 21-foot (6.4-meter) diameter of the round gardens creates a surface area of 346 square feet (32.2 square meters).

3. Review and discuss the information from the "Bridges: From Legends to Life" section of this chapter. The rest of this activity description explains how to make two kinds of Three Sisters Gardens: a Wampanoag Three Sisters Garden from the Eastern Woodlands, and a traditional Hidatsa Garden from the Plains.

4. Remember to plant extra amounts of each crop to share some with the raccoons, crows and other animals.

5. Use your gardening experience and the information in both Chapter 3 and the "Bridges" section of this chapter to explore these concepts:

- the circle of planter and crop, giving and receiving

- the cycle of gardening seasons (planting, hoeing, ripening, harvesting) and celebration during the moons of the growing season (many Native cultures plant their seeds when the moon is *waxing,* or growing full)

- the circle of birth, life and death in the garden

- sharing the garden with insects and animals that also eat the crop

- the importance of considering local climate and length of growing season when choosing seeds

- the idea of "weeds"

- soil fertility: compost, green manure, legumes, nitrogen fixing and soil enrichment

- soil and water conservation: green manures, mulching, raised fields, terracing, etc.

- the benefits of companion planting

- traditional "Three Sisters" agriculture of corn, beans and squash and the advantages of this system over modern monoculture

- the balanced ecosystem formed by traditional Three Sisters Garden crops

- the environmental benefits of this approach to gardening, such as avoiding water pollution from fertilizer running off into waterways and preventing problems associated with pesticide use

- gardening and re-creation, rejuvenation

### WAMPANOAG THREE SISTERS GARDEN[18]
The traditional Wampanoag garden includes corn, beans, squash (summer and winter squash and pumpkin) and sunflower. Each traditional family needed to grow about 1 acre of crops to supply their needs for food from the garden. Weeding is usually done with a hoe. Harvesting takes place throughout the season as the different varieties of crops ripen. Large traditional gardens of 2 to 3 acres (.8 to 1.2 hectares) relied on the

*Corn, beans and squash growing in the young Wampanoag garden.*

rains because they were too large to be watered by hand. Extra amounts of each crop were also planted to share with the animals.

### Corn

1. Measure the size of your garden plot and outline the garden on a piece of paper. Look at the illustrations of the Wampanoag garden and lay out the pattern of corn mounds as they will fit in your garden. Allow 4 feet (1.2 meters) between the *centers* of the mounds.

*Planting design for the Wampanoag garden: square version. See the text for exact sizes, arrangements and distances between crop mounds. Also see the illustrations that follow showing how to create and plant the mounds containing both corn and beans as well as the squash mounds. (scale: 1 inch = 4.7 feet {1 centimeter = .56 meters}.)*

c = corn        b = bean        sq = squash        sf = sunflower

2. As soon as the soil is ready to be worked, create the corn mound pattern and spacing in your garden that you have designed on paper. Use small sticks to mark the locations of the centers of all the mounds.

3. Build up the mounds. This is a lot of fun—sort of like sculpting. Each mound measures about 18 inches (46 centimeters) across at the base and 10 inches (25 centimeters) across the flat top where the corn will be planted. Mounds are about 4 inches (10 centimeters) tall. Although it is not traditional, we like to create a depression with a lip on it surrounding the flat top of each mound to retain water. Traditionally, mounds build up gradually over the years as soil is hoed up around the growing cornstalks to provide support.

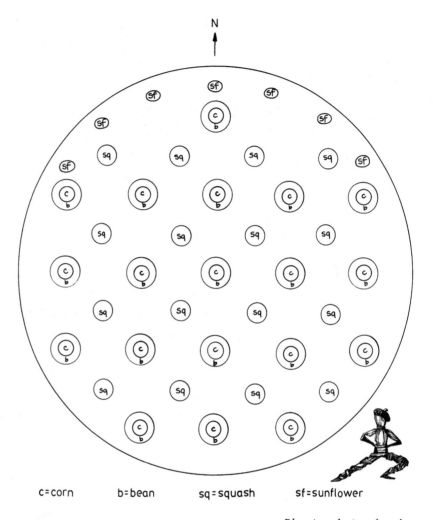

c = corn    b = bean    sq = squash    sf = sunflower

*Planting design for the Wampanoag garden: round version. (scale: 1 inch = 5 feet {1 centimeter = .59 meters}.)*

4. Plant the corn seeds. Traditionally, the Wampanoag corn is planted when the leaves on the dogwood or shadblow (Juneberry or serviceberry) trees are the size of a squirrel's ear. You may want to use the traditional northern eight-row flint corn of Wampanoag gardens as well as the other Native varieties you have chosen. Whatever kinds of corn you plant, the seeds of each variety should be planted close together in the garden so that they can pollinate themselves. If several varieties are planted, set them out so that they ripen from east to west, in the same direction the sun travels. This will also help

*Tending the Wampanoag Three Sisters Garden.*

you later on when you
are trying to remem-
ber which varieties
ripen first.

A healthy young
ear of corn is capped
with *silks* and grows
out of the stalk at the
base of some leaves.
Ears and silks are the
female parts of the
corn plant. Each fertil-
ized strand of silk
forms a single kernel
of corn on the ear. Dif-
ferent strands of silk
can be fertilized by
pollen from different
male flowers, called
*tassels,* found atop the
cornstalks.

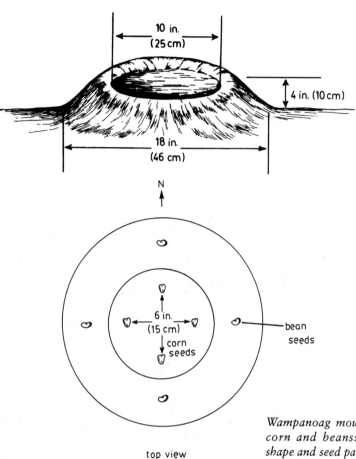

top view

*Wampanoag mound of corn and beans: size, shape and seed patterns. Corn seeds are planted in the flat top of each mound. Beans seeds are planted halfway down the slopes on the sides of each mound.*

Traditionally, each
variety of corn is planted in its own separate field so that the
varieties do not cross-pollinate. It is difficult to isolate corn varieties completely unless you plant them in separate garden plots.
The best you can do in a small garden is to plant only a few varieties, and locate the seeds of each variety in mounds that are close
together. We look forward to getting some cross-pollination in
the garden. Ears of corn from our yellow varieties often end up
with a few colorful kernels from other, different-colored kinds of
corn growing nearby.

Like many Native North Americans, the Wampanoag people
often give thanks each day to the Four Directions while they
are in the garden. Some Native people today like to honor this
tradition by planting to the Four Directions. Use the sun or a
compass to find north, south, east and west. The sun rises in
the east, sets in the west and appears above the southern hori-
zon at mid-day. Orient the corn seeds to the Four Directions as
you plant them on top of the mounds. Make four holes on top
of each mound about 6 inches (15 centimeters) apart when

measuring across the center of the mound. Plant one seed in each hole. Plant the seeds about 3 inches (8 centimeters) deep or as deep as the instructions on the seed packet indicate.

5. Weed the corn when it grows to the height of a hand, about 6 inches (15 centimeters). Weed again every few weeks.

6. Once the cornstalks grow to be a few feet (about 60 centimeters) high, draw up some soil around the base of the stalks for support.

7. Some corn can be harvested in August as "green corn" or sweet corn. At this stage the corn is juicy and sweet. It is good for cooking to eat out of hand or for making into succotash (see the recipe for succotash in Chapter 5).

Later, in September or early October, depending on your climate, the corn will have matured on the stalks. When you harvest the ears of corn, leave the stalks in place to support the beans. Pull the corn husks back and braid them together with those of other ears of corn to form a long *rope*. Hang these ropes of corn overhead and out of the rain to dry. Drying can also be done on mats, which are traditionally woven from cattails. Any dry mat will do.

Traditionally, all corn is dried on the cob. In the Northeast, once the corn is dried, *seed corn* is stored on the cob while *feed corn* is *shelled*—removed from the cob—for easy storage. Feed corn is then stored in baskets that hold about 3 to 4 bushels (106 to 141 liters). In the past, corn was stored in pits lined with grass and bark that held about 8 bushels (282 liters). Dried corn husks are traditionally used for making baskets and mats. In the arid Southwest, corn is usually stored on the cob until just before it is used.

Do not forget to put some piles of cracked corn around the garden, but away from it, so that the local wild animals will not eat too much of your crop.

### Beans

1. Wait until the corn grows to at least the height of a finger (about 4 inches [10 centimeters]) before planting the beans. This takes about two weeks in good growing weather. Be patient. If the beans are planted too early, the vines will overrun the young corn plants and smother them. If this begins

to happen, you can gently prune away the bean vines that are covering the young corn, but leave enough beans for a good crop.

A total of four bean seeds are planted in four separate holes made about one-half of the way down the sloped side of each mound. These seeds may also be aligned with the Four Directions. Kidney, navy, pea and pinto beans are traditionally used by the Wampanoag. These varieties of the common bean (*Phaseolus vulgaris*) are pole or climbing beans that use the cornstalks for support. Other Native varieties include snap beans and the Mexican frijole.

2. Some beans may be picked as immature or *green beans*. Be sure to leave enough bean pods to provide a good harvest when they mature. Beans are mature when the pods turn brown. This is when they can be shelled or removed from the pod and dried.

### Squash

1. Plant the squash at the same time as the beans. Once the squash sprout, the large leaves cast deep shade over everything beneath them. This helps control weeds, but make sure that the squash leaves do not smother young corn and bean seedlings as well. Build up some rounded mounds in the open spaces *between* the mounds of corn and beans. Each mound should be about a foot (30 centimeters) across at the base and 3 inches (7.6 centimeters) high.

2. Squash should be planted four seeds to each rounded mound, and can be aligned to the Four Directions. Leave about 8 inches (20 centimeters) in between the seeds as measured across the center of each mound. Plant both summer and winter varieties of squash, including pumpkin, acorn and summer

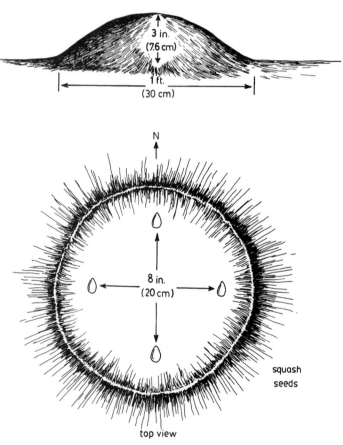

*Wampanoag squash mound: size, shape and seed pattern.*

crookneck. Other varieties that are probably traditional are turban squash, hubbard and bush scallop.

3. If you want to grow gourds, plant those seeds around the edges of several of the squash mounds at this time. Make sure to mark the locations of the gourd seeds. See the "*Growing, Drying and Finishing Gourds*" activity later in this chapter.

4. Harvest the summer squash and, later, the winter squash varieties when they are ready. Chapter 5 explains how to prepare squash and pumpkin seeds to eat. Be sure to save some seeds to dry for next year's planting. Clean these seeds and air-dry them on large, flat pans set out in a dry space.

### Sunflower

1. Sunflowers are often planted around the edge of the garden at the same time as the corn. You will want to plant the sunflowers along the north side of the garden so that they will not cast shade over the other crops. Traditionally, the common sunflower (*Helianthus annuus*) is planted, not the familiar giant sunflower. Make some small mounds about 3 feet (1 meter) apart and plant three seeds in each mound.

2. Leave the ripe seeds on the sunflower heads until they harden and take on the color of that particular variety. We usually leave the seeds on the flower heads until around the time of the first frost, but watch carefully to make sure that the birds do not beat you to the harvest!

### HIDATSA THREE SISTERS GARDEN[19]

The Hidatsa are a people of the plains who live in what is now North Dakota. Buffalo Bird Woman, whose Hidatsa name is *Maxidiwiac,* was born in 1839. Her garden, which was located along the floodplain of the Missouri River, was typical of those found among the Hidatsa, Mandan and Arikara peoples. In addition to corn, beans, squash and sunflower, tobacco was grown, but in separate plots. The same hills were used for planting each year, but each garden plot was rotated periodically and left fallow for two years so that the soil could replenish itself.

*Blooms of the native common sunflower* (Helianthus annuus).

### Sunflower

**1.** Choose the round or square version of the Hidatsa Three Sisters Garden. Measure and plan your garden space to suit the design you have chosen.

**2.** As soon as the soil can be worked and the danger of frost is past, build up some small hills on the north side of the garden. This way, the tall sunflowers will not cast shade on the other crops. Space the hills in a row about 3 feet (1 meter) apart. Although sunflowers were traditionally planted about "eight or nine paces apart," this was done in gardens much larger than the one described here.

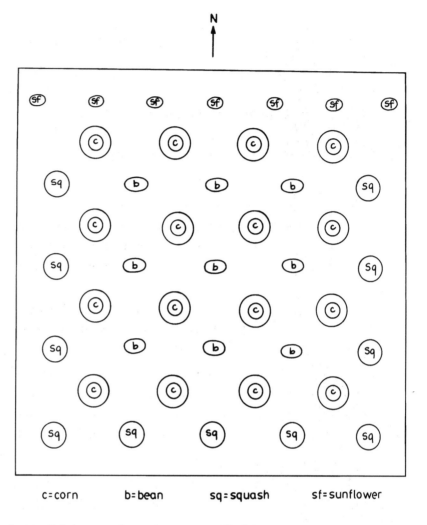

c=corn   b=bean   sq=squash   sf=sunflower

*Planting design for the Hidatsa garden: square version. See the text for exact sizes, arrangements and distances between crop mounds. Also see the illustrations that follow showing how to create and plant the mounds of sunflowers, corn, beans and squash. (scale: 1 inch = 4.7 feet {1 centimeter = .56 meters}.)*

**3.** Plant three sunflower seeds per hill. All three seeds are planted in the same hole on each hill. Hidatsa varieties of sunflower traditionally produce seeds that are black, white, red and striped.

   **Note:** At this time you will need to plant your squash seeds indoors in the peat pots and seed flats. Once they have sprouted, the squash seedlings will be put out in the garden a few weeks

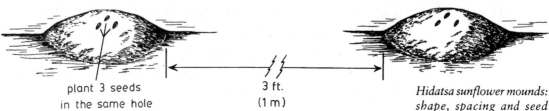

plant 3 seeds
in the same hole
atop each hill

3 ft.
(1 m)

*Hidatsa sunflower mounds: shape, spacing and seed placement.*

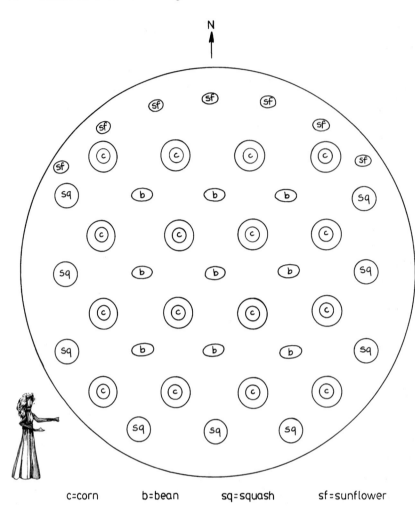

c=corn    b=bean    sq=squash    sf=sunflower

*Planting design for the Hidatsa garden: round version. (scale: 1 inch = 5 feet {1 centimeter = .59 meter}.)*

after the corn and beans have been planted. Gourd seeds can also be started at this time, if you wish. See the "Planting, Watering and Growing" section in Chapter 3 for tips on managing seedlings.

**Corn**

1. Look at the illustration and lay out the pattern of corn mounds as they will fit in your garden. Note that the mounds of corn are in line with each other, but they are staggered compared to the mounds of beans. Allow 4 feet (1.2 meters) between the *centers* of the corn mounds. Leave a strip of garden space around the east, south and west edges of the garden where the squash will be planted. Traditionally, there are four rows of corn between each row of squash or sunflowers in the garden.

2. Wait a week or two after the sunflowers have been planted so that the soil has a chance to begin drying out. Corn seeds are apt to rot in wet soil. Create the corn mound pattern and spacing in your garden that you have designed on paper by using small sticks to mark the locations of the centers of all the mounds.

3. Build up the corn mounds. Each mound measures about 18 inches (46 centimeters) across at the base and 9 inches (23 centimeters) across the flat top where the corn will be planted. Mounds are about 4 inches (10 centimeters) tall.

Although it is not a Hidatsa tradition, you can create a rim of soil around the edge of the top of each corn mound in order to make watering easier.

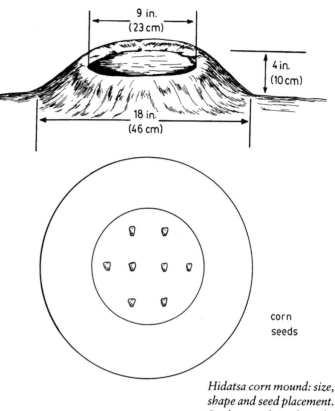

4. Plant the corn seeds. Traditionally, the Hidatsa flint corn is planted in May in North Dakota, when the leaves on the wild gooseberry bushes are almost fully formed. You should plant a week or two after the soil is ready to plant in your climate (see "Preparing and Maintaining the Soil" in Chapter 3). Use a traditional flint corn plus the other Native varieties you acquired in the *"Native Seeds"* activity. The

*Hidatsa corn mound: size, shape and seed placement. Seeds are planted in the flat top of each mound.*

Hidatsa use a semiarid variety of flint corn, but you will need to choose varieties of corn that suit your growing conditions. Whatever kinds of corn you plant, the seeds of each variety should be planted close together in the garden so that they can pollinate themselves. If several varieties are planted, set them out so that they ripen from east to west, in the same direction that the sun travels. This also helps you later on when you are trying to remember which varieties ripen first.

Plant eight corn seeds on the flat top of each mound according to the pattern shown in the illustration.

5. When harvesting the corn, be sure to leave the stalks intact to support the beans that are twined around them.

### Beans

1. Build up the bean hills in the open spaces between the mounds of corn. The bean hills are in line with one another, but are staggered compared to the rows of corn. The rounded bean hills are ovals measuring 7 inches (18 centimeters) wide by 14 inches (36 centimeters) long.

*The traditional Hidatsa Garden in full growth.*

2. Plant the bean seeds immediately after planting the corn. Plant two groups of bean seeds per hill on the south-facing side of the mound as shown in the illustration. There are three or four bean seeds in each group, with 6 inches (15 centimeters) between the two groups in each mound.

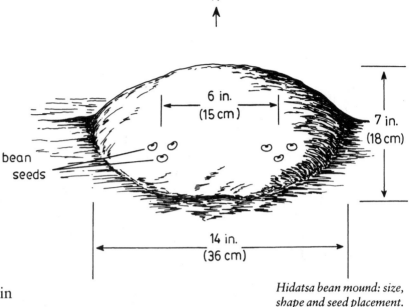

*Hidatsa bean mound: size, shape and seed placement.*

### Squash

1. Mound up the squash hills in the strip of soil that lies along the east, south and west sides of the garden. Line them up with the ends of the bean rows, 4 feet (1.2 meters) away, as shown in the illustration. You will also need to leave 4 feet (1.2 meters) between the centers of the squash mounds. Each mound will measure about 15 inches (38 centimeters) across at the base.

2. Plant the squash seedlings (which you began earlier) about two weeks after you have planted the corn and beans, once the other crops have sprouted. In North Dakota, this is late May or early June. The four squash seed-

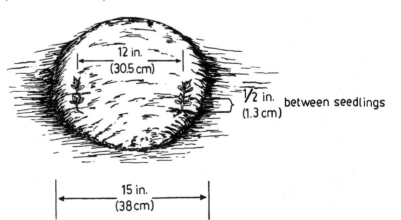

lings planted per hill are set out as two pairs on the south-facing slope. There should be 12 inches (30.5 centimeters) between each pair. A half-inch (1.3-centimeter) space should be left between the stems of the seedlings in each pair.

3. If you have sprouted gourd seeds, set out those seedlings at this time. Plant the seedlings along the edges of some of the

*Hidatsa squash mound: size, shape and placement of the seedlings. Two pairs of seedlings are planted 12 inches (30.5 centimeters) apart. Leave 1/2 inch (1.3 centimeters) between the seedlings within each pair.*

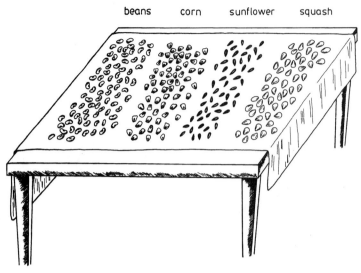

beans    corn    sunflower    squash

*Lay the seeds out to dry in a clean, dry, well-ventilated place.*

squash mounds. See the *"Growing, Drying and Finishing Gourds"* activity later in this chapter.

## Co-Kokopilau: Keepers of the Seeds

**ACTIVITY:** Harvest ripe seeds from each of the crops in your garden. Preserve them for the winter and for planting next spring.

**MATERIALS:** Enough seeds from each of the crops in your garden to plant a new crop next year; clean old sheets; enough small, clean, dry glass jars (the kind used for preserves) with rubber-sealed lids so that you have one for each kind of seed you want to save; sticky labels for the jars; pen.

**DIGGING IN:**

1. Reread the end of the "Bridges: From Legends to Life" section where it tells of Kokopilau, the Hump-Backed Flute Player. Like Kokopilau, you are going to store the seeds from your garden and take care of them until it is time to plant again next year.

2. Gather seeds from each of your crops as they ripen. When a vegetable is ripe, the seeds are also ready to harvest and begin drying. If you have questions about how to handle the seeds of a particular crop, see the directions given in the crop descriptions of the Wampanoag Three Sisters Garden activity. Make sure you have enough seeds to plant a new crop next year.

3. Clean the seeds of any remnants of dried flower parts, husks, stalks, capsules and other matter that may still be clinging to them.

4. Lay the seeds out on the old sheets in a clean, dry, well-ventilated place for a few weeks until they are dry and hard.

5. Place the seeds from each crop in a preserving jar of their own and screw the cap on securely until sealed.

6. Label each jar as you fill it. Include on the label: the name of the crop the seed is from, whose garden it was grown in, the date of storage and who is storing the seed.

7. Store the seeds in a cool, dark, dry place until you need them next growing season.

# Native Garden Crafts

## Activities

Make rattles, storage jars, birdhouses and other projects from gourds. Create your own corn husk dolls. Make a scarecrow adapted from a Hidatsa design.

## Growing, Drying and Finishing Gourds

**MATERIALS:** Seeds for a mixed variety of ornamental gourds, seeds of the bottle gourd (*Lagenaria vulgaris*) and/or "birdhouse gourd," pruning shears, steel wool or other scouring pad.

**DIGGING IN:**

**1.** Gourd projects are a great way to extend the garden experience through indoor activities during the long winter season. To begin, plant a variety of gourds in your garden at the same time that you set out the squash (gourds are closely related to squash). Plant them along the edges of a few of the squash mounds. Gourd seeds often come in packages that contain a mix of varieties. We enjoy being surprised by the different gourds that appear in our garden.

In addition to the ornamental gourds that gardeners normally plant, however, you will need to plant some other varieties for the gourd activities. Make sure that you plant some bottle gourds (*Lagenaria vulgaris*) and birdhouse gourds, which grow larger than most and will be used for bottles and birdhouses in other activities. You can find seeds for these large, sturdy gourds in seed catalogs and local seed stores, or you can obtain them from the American Gourd Society, P.O. Box 274, Mount Gilead, OH, 43338-0274; (419) 362-6446. The American Gourd Society publishes a quarterly newsletter and sells seeds in packets.

As gourd plants grow, they form vines that trail along the ground and climb up the cornstalks. Be sure to leave a piece of stem on each ripened gourd as you prune it from the vine.

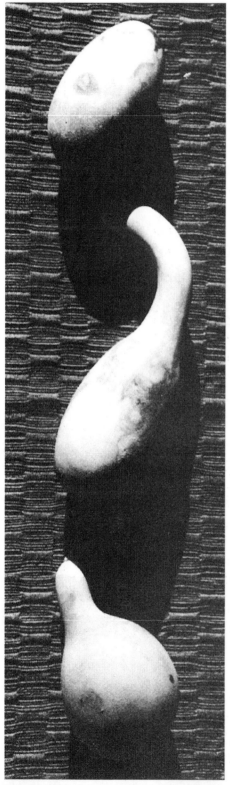

*Dried gourds that are ready to use for making rattles. Notice the mold stains which often form even when the gourds are cured in a dry, sunny, well-aerated place.*

2. Begin to *dry* and *cure* the gourds immediately after harvest. This is a slow process that often takes several months. In order to reduce molding and rotting, lay the gourds out on a flat surface with space between each gourd. A dry, well-aerated space with plenty of sunshine is best (not a damp cellar!). It is normal for some mold to form on the outside of the gourds as they are drying. Do not throw gourds away if they get a bit moldy, so long as they are keeping their shape. The only gourds that you will need to remove and compost are those that start to shrivel. You will know a gourd is ready when the outside has dried into a hard shell that sounds hollow when you tap it. Also, the fresh gourds, that can weigh as much as 10 pounds (4.5 kilograms) or more, become very light when dried—they weigh only a fraction of what they weighed at harvest. Finally, when you shake the gourd vigorously but carefully, the seeds inside will often begin to rattle.

3. *Finish* the outside of the dried gourds. Let them sit in the rain for the better part of a day until the skin softens up a bit, then use a non-soapy scouring pad to *gently* rub away the skin and smooth the outside. Do not rub too hard or the gourd will become scratched. Allow the gourds to dry thoroughly once more. Finished gourds look like wood without the grain.

## Gourd Rattles

**MATERIALS:** A variety of dried and finished gourds, water-based art paint that becomes waterproof when dry, containers for water and paint, paintbrushes, newspaper for drop cloth and rags for cleaning up.

**DIGGING IN:**

1. Choose some dried, finished gourds. Use small dried gourds that have begun to rattle when you shake them. Gourds with long, narrow necks work well because they have natural handles. Or,

you may want to choose a round gourd that fits just right in the palm of your hand. Any gourd will do as a rattle.

2. Now paint your favorite designs on the gourds to create the rattles. You can also paint pictures that tell the story of your garden.

## Gourd Storage Jars

MATERIALS: Bottle gourds (dried and finished), pencil, fine-toothed handsaw (coping saw or hacksaw), work gloves, dried corncob for stopper, medium and fine grit sandpaper, pliers, bent piece of coat hanger, paint and supplies (as in the *"Gourd Rattles"* activity) or other art materials, if desired, for decorating the gourds.

DIGGING IN:

1. Choose some of the larger bottle gourds to use for making jars. These should be dried and finished on the outside. Use a pencil to mark a line where you want to cut off the top of the gourd. The size of the opening should be right for the size of the stopper you will use.

2. Wear the work gloves while you saw. Working very carefully with a fine-toothed handsaw (*young children should be supervised for this task*), cut along this line across the top of the neck of the gourd where you want to make the opening.

3. Use a bent piece of coat hanger with a loop on the tip to gently scrape away and break up the dried-out seeds and flesh from the inside of the gourd. Pull the pieces out of the hole and be careful not to crack the shell. Be sure to save the seeds for drying and planting next year.

4. Sand the lip of the opening with the fine sandpaper until smooth.

5. Slip the narrow end of the corncob into the mouth of the gourd jar to see which section fits snugly. Keep trying it out as you sand and shape. Hold one end of the corncob as you use the medium sandpaper to smooth and shape it into a stopper. The stopper will be tapered, with the narrow end going into the top of the gourd jar first.

6. Now use the handsaw to trim the stopper off from the rest of the corncob. Cut the stopper in two places: about 1 inch

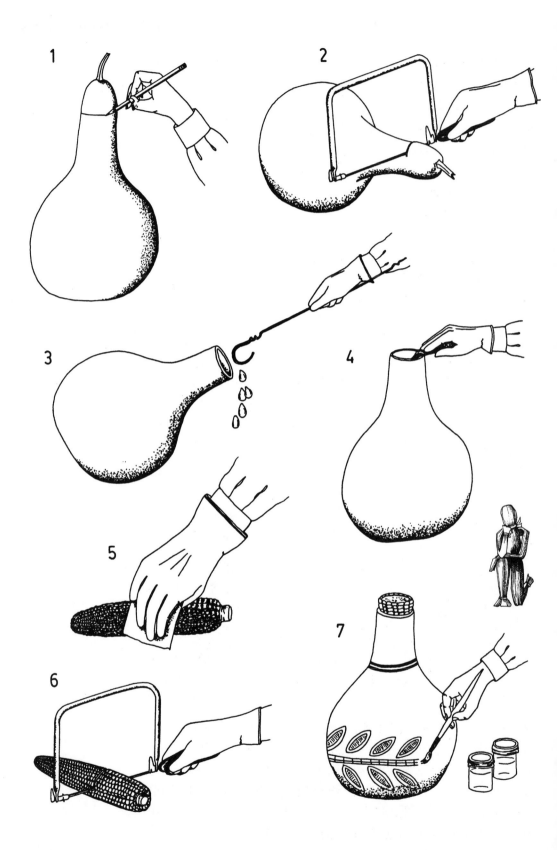

*Making a gourd storage jar. Directions for each numbered step are given in the text.*
*This jar is adorned with a Cherokee design.*

(2.5 centimeters) above and 1 inch (2.5 centimeters) below where the corncob fits snugly in the gourd jar. The stopper will be about 2 inches (5 centimeters) long. Sand the newly cut edges of the stopper and insert it into the mouth of the jar.

7. Decorate the outside to complete your gourd bottle.

## Gourd Birdhouses

**MATERIALS:** Birdhouse and/or bottle gourds (dried and finished), pencil, drill, quarter-inch (.6-centimeter) drill bit, safety eyeglasses (if you are using a power drill), ruler, blade from a fine-toothed handsaw (coping saw), masking tape, work gloves, fine sandpaper, pliers, bent piece of coat hanger, paint and supplies (as in the *"Gourd Rattles"* activity) if desired, sturdy piece of wire for hanging the birdhouse, tape measure.

**DIGGING IN:** Birdhouses can attract many different kinds of cavity-nesting birds to the garden. Not only are they colorful, lively and full of song, birds also eat a lot of insects that harm garden plants. Birds become very territorial when nesting, and some will even chase away crows, magpies and other large birds that might eat the corn you are growing. For this reason, some Native people used to put up birdhouses to attract purple martins to the garden.

1. Choose a dried and finished bottle gourd or birdhouse gourd that is about the right size for the kind of bird you want to attract to your garden. The chart, "Gourd Birdhouse Specifications," on page 100 provides the sizes for houses and doorways that some common birds prefer.

2. Use a pencil to outline the hole you want to make in the side of the gourd. The chart also tells you how big a hole to make for the kind of bird you want to attract. You should locate the hole a bit below the middle of the "belly" of the gourd where it begins to curve in toward the bottom. That way the entranceway faces down a bit and will not catch rainwater.

3. Wear the work gloves as you work. In addition, put on the safety glasses if you are using a power drill. Carefully drill a

*Gourd birdhouse.*

## Gourd Birdhouse Specifications

| Species | Entrance diameter (inches) | Entrance above bottom of gourd (inches) | Floor dimensions (inches) | House depth (inches) | Nest above ground (feet) |
|---|---|---|---|---|---|
| Bluebird | $1^1/_2$ | 6–7 | 5x5 | 8–9 | 4–10 |
| Chickadee, | | | | | |
|    black-capped | $1^1/_8$ | 6–8 | 4x4 | 8–12 | 5–50 |
| Flycatcher, | | | | | |
|    great crested | 2 | 6–8 | 6x6 | 8–10 | 8–20 |
| Martin, purple | $2^1/_2$ | 2 | 7x7 | 7 | 8–16 |
| Owl, saw-whet | $2^1/_2$ | 8–10 | 6x6 | 10–12 | 12–20 |
| Phoebe | open sides | | 6x6 | 6 | 8–12 |
| Robin | open front | | 6x8 | 8 | 6–15 |
| Sapsucker | $1^3/_4$ | 12–16 | 6x6 | 14–18 | 12–40 |
| Swallow | | | | | |
|    barn | open sides | | 6x6 | 6 | 8–12 |
|    tree | $1^1/_2$ | 1–5 | 5x5 | 6 | 10–15 |
| Titmouse, tufted | $1^1/_4$ | 6–8 | 4x4 | 8–10 | 4–15 |
| Woodpecker | | | | | |
|    downy | $1^1/_4$ | 6–8 | 4x4 | 8–10 | 6–20 |
|    hairy | $1^1/_2$ | 9–12 | 6x6 | 12–16 | 12–20 |
|    red-bellied | $2^1/_2$ | 10–12 | 6x6 | 12–14 | 12–50 |
|    red-headed | 2 | 9–12 | 6x6 | 12–15 | 12–100 |
| Wren | | | | | |
|    Bewick's | $1^1/_4$ | 6–8 | 4x4 | 4–6 | 6–10 |
|    Carolina | $1^1/_4$ | 4–6 | 4x4 | 4–6 | 5–12 |
|    house | $1–1^1/_4$ | 6–8 | 4x4 | 4–6 | 5–10 |
|    winter | $1–1^1/_4$ | 6–8 | 4x4 | 4–8 | 5–10 |

hole along the *inside* edge of the circle which will become the doorway. This hole must be large enough so that the end of the coping saw blade can pass through. Use masking tape to cover up one end of the coping saw blade. Now, using a gloved hand, hold the taped part of the saw blade and slip a few inches (5 centimeters) of the other end in through the hole you drilled earlier. Carefully and patiently cut along the circular line you marked to create the doorway. *(It is not necessary to scrape away the dried seeds and other material from the inside of the gourd. The birds will do this as they prepare to nest in your gourd birdhouse.)*

**4.** Use the fine sandpaper to carefully round out and smooth the lip of the doorway.

5. While you have the drill handy, make three holes in the very bottom of the gourd for drainage. Each hole should be about 1 inch (2.5 centimeters) from the center of the bottom of the gourd. The three holes should be an equal distance from each other, forming a triangle.

6. In order to hang the birdhouse, use the drill to make a hole about 2 inches (5 centimeters) from the top. Cut the hole from side to side directly through the center of the gourd. Slip some sturdy wire through this hole and bend the ends up and together to form a hanger. Check the chart for the correct height to hang the gourd birdhouse.

## Corn Husk Dolls

**MATERIALS:** Fresh green corn husks (about eight pieces to make each doll), bowl of water and a clean absorbent rag (optional), sharp scissors, white nontoxic glue, corn silk, acorn caps or other nutshells for caps. If used carefully, the husks from one ear of corn will make two small dolls.

**DIGGING IN:**

1. Carefully peel back the husks from a large, fresh ear of corn. Try not to tear each sheath of husk as you pull it back. Husks often turn brown at the tip. Trim any brown tips away. If the husks are green and pliable, you can use them as is. If they have dried out somewhat and become stiff, soak the husks in water for an hour or two, then blot them dry.

2. Tear one corn husk lengthwise into thin strips. Use these strips as cord for tying.

3. Roll a piece of corn husk lengthwise, then tie and trim the ends. This piece will become the arms of the corn husk doll.

4. Take two pieces of corn husk and tear each piece lengthwise into four parts of equal width.

5. Gather these eight pieces into a bundle with all the

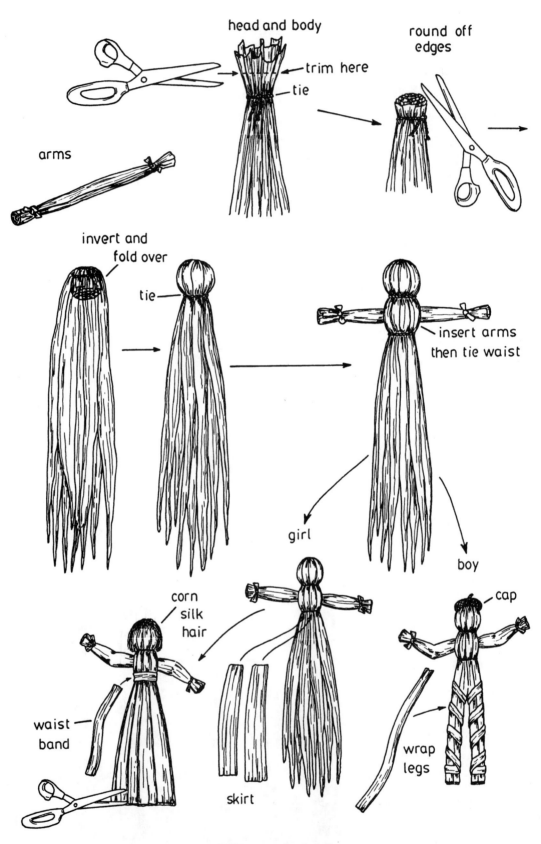

scissors

head and body
trim here
tie

round off
edges

arms

invert and
fold over
tie

insert arms
then tie waist

girl

boy

corn
silk
hair

cap

waist
band

skirt

wrap
legs

*Making corn husk dolls.*

thicker parts of the husks positioned evenly at one end (the thicker parts were attached to the bottom of the ear of corn). Tie this bundle tightly about 2 inches (5 centimeters) down from that end. Trim the thick ends of the husks off even with one another about 3/4 inch (2 centimeters) above where you have tied them together. This little bulb of husks will become the *inside* of the head. Use the scissors to round off the edges of the bulb a bit.

6. Turn the whole bundle over. Now invert the long pieces of husk down and bend them over the bulb you created earlier. Gather these husks in tightly under the bulb and tie them off to form the neck. Arrange (do not cut) the husks around the bulb to shape the round head and create a smooth face.

7. Slip the arms in underneath the sheaths of corn husks that are hanging beneath the neck. Tie a piece of husk cord below the arms to form the waist and hold the arms in place.

8. If you are making a boy, separate the husks that are hanging down into two equal-sized bundles, one for each leg. Use a wide strip of husk to wrap around each bundle to form pants, and tie these off to form the ankles. Trim the ends of both legs off evenly below the ankles.

9. To make a girl doll wearing a dress, use several pieces of husk cut from the ends that pointed toward the top of the ear of corn. Cut a little bit of the point off each piece of husk. Place the narrow pointed ends of these husks around the doll's waist and arrange the husks to form a skirt. Put a drop of glue under the tip of each husk at the waist to hold it in place. Wrap a corn husk tie several times around the upper ends of these husks to hold them in place and form a waistband. Tie this waistband firmly in place. Neatly trim the bottom edge of the dress with a pair of scissors at the place that would mark the bottom of the feet.

10. Carefully bend the arms down a little at the shoulders and bend them in a bit at the elbows.

11. Now use your imagination to finish the dolls: use dried corn silk for hair, add some acorn caps for hats and so on. *Traditional corn husk dolls do not have facial features.*

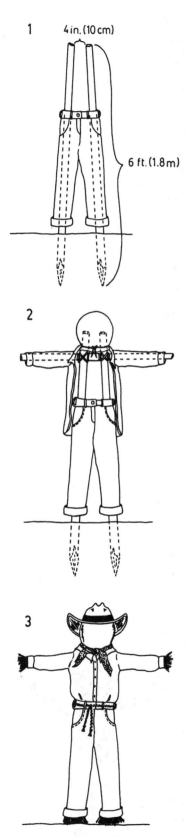

*Making a scarecrow.*

## Scarecrow

**MATERIALS:** Work gloves, small bow saw, tape measure, two dead branches measuring 6 feet (1.8 meters) long by 2 inches (5 centimeters) thick, one branch measuring 5.5 feet (1.7 meters) long by 1.5 inches (3.8 centimeters) thick, hatchet, mallet, lightweight rope, trousers or dress (or old sheet for a dress), old shirt, old sheet for the head, sharp scissors, string, safety pins, dried leaves and/or hay for stuffing, hat, paint, buttons, sewing needle, thread and other supplies as desired for other details.

**DIGGING IN:** There are many ways to make a scarecrow. Some traditional scarecrows, such as those of the Zuni, are very detailed. Although they scare the crows away only for a day or two until the birds see that the "person" is never moving, scarecrows are fun to make and have around. Following are simple directions for making a scarecrow modeled after a Hidatsa design.

**1.** Cut two dead pieces of branch about 6 feet (1.8 meters) long and 2 inches (5 centimeters) thick. Cut another dead stick measuring 5.5 feet (1.7 meters) long by 1.5 inches (3.8 centimeters) thick.

**2.** Make a point on one end of each of the two longer branches. Pound these points about 8 inches (20 centimeters) into the ground as you angle the sticks so that the tops lean toward one another. The distance *between* the tops of the leg branches should be about 4 inches (10 centimeters). These two sticks will serve as the legs and body.

**3.** If you want to make a scarecrow wearing pants, you will now need to slip the cuffs of an old pair of trousers down over the upper ends of the leg sticks before attaching the arms.

**4.** Slip the third branch through the arms of an old shirt or dress. Now tie the third stick across near the top of the two leg branches to form arms of equal length. Leave about 8 inches (20 centimeters) of the tops of the leg branches sticking up above the level where the arm branch is tied across them. The tops of the leg branches that stick up above where the arm branch crosses will form the neck attachment for the head.

**5.** If you do not have a worn-out dress to spare and you want to make a female scarecrow, drape an old sheet around the scarecrow for a dress. If the scarecrow wears pants, you will need to use safety pins to attach the trousers over and around the waist area of the shirt.

**6.** Fill a piece of cloth with leaves and fashion it into a ball for the head. Wrap the rope snugly around the neck to form the ball, but do not tie it off yet. Slip the open end of the ball of leaves down over the neck sticks and tie the rope off around the neck to hold the head on.

**7.** Stuff the scarecrow clothes with hay or leaves, then tie a rope around it for a waistband. Push some hay up into the ends of the arms and bottoms of the pant legs to form hands and feet.

**8.** Add a hat to finish the scarecrow. *As with traditional corn husk dolls, scarecrows do not have facial features.*

## Branching Out

- Make up a tune to go with the song that Bean Woman sings in the Tutelo story "The Bean Woman." Make up another song to be the one Grasshopper sings in the Zuni story "The Grasshopper's Song." Sing these songs and other soothing music to the Native plants that grow in your garden.

- Reread the Tuscarora story "Onenha, The Corn" from Chapter 1. Put some music to the words of thanksgiving in the song that the ears of corn sing as they hang on the drying pole of the man's lodge. Sing this song to the corn as it grows.

- Use your gourd rattles to accompany your music or any other songs you like. A wonderful book and tape set to use as a source of Native American music is *Moving Within the Circle: Contemporary Native American Music and Dance* by Bryan Burton (Danbury, Conn.: World Music Press, 1993).

- At the end of "The Bean Woman," she throws her arms around Corn Man's neck. As your Three Sisters Garden grows, watch for the Bean Woman to "twine her arms around the corn in a loving way."

- Reread the parts of the "Bridges: From Legends to Life" section of this chapter that explain why the Three Sisters of Corn, Beans and Squash are such good companion plants in the Native garden. Create your own puppet show, play or story about the adventures of the Three Sisters in your garden.

- In the story "The Grasshopper's Song," Grasshopper says he will give his garden to the boy if the boy agrees to save the seeds and plant them next year in the garden so that Grasshopper will have a home. Go around your garden and find the insects and animals that are living there. Draw pictures of the garden places that are homes for these animals. Create your own story about a garden that is somebody's home, and explain what happens when someone else wants to use that garden.

- Read the Arikara story "Sharing the Corn" in Chapter 5. The bull buffalo in this story faces in the Four Directions, and four different colors of corn form on the stalk that grows where the bull buffalo stood. Draw a picture of a cornstalk bearing ears in these four colors, In honor of the four colors and the Four Directions, the Arikara plant four corn seeds in each mound. Seeds in the Wampanoag Three Sisters Garden can also be planted to honor the Four Directions. Many Native Americans give thanks to the Four Directions for the gifts of life from their gardens. Look for the number four to appear in other Native stories.

- Make a list of all the things we get from corn. Read the article "Corn: The Golden Grain" by Robert E. Rhoades, in *National Geographic,* vol. 183, no. 6 (June 1993), pages 92–117. Some of the products from corn are cornmeal, cornstarch, corn oil, corn syrup, corn silage for animal feed, paper, wallboard, fuel, fertilizer, plastics, adhesives, felts, cleaning compounds, cosmetics, drugs, alcohol and soaps. (Thanks to Jean Minnich for this idea.)

- Have fun with the information and activities relating corn and Three Sisters gardening in the April 1994 issue of *Growing Ideas* (vol. 5, no. 2), which is available from the National Gardening Association, 180 Flynn Avenue, Burlington, VT 05401.

- In order to become more knowledgeable about, and involved with, saving seeds, read the excellent reference book *Seed to Seed* by Suzanne Ashworth (Decorah, Iowa: Seed Saver Pub., 1991). Available from: Chelsea Green Publishing Co., P.O. Box 428, White River Junction, VT 05001; (800) 639-4099.

- Visit other people's gardens. Invite others to your garden and share your food.

- Celebrate plants using the story and activities in Chapter 4 of *Keepers of Life*.

- Read the Cherokee story "The Coming of Corn" in Chapter 16 of *Keepers of the Earth*.

- Read the Hopi story "Kokopilau, The Hump-Backed Flute Player" in Chapter 18 of *Keepers of the Earth*.

- Notice the "weed" species growing in your garden. Try to identify and learn about these plants. Find out where they grow in the wild and whether they are native to North America.

- Experiment and create new corn varieties. Shake the pollen from the male flowers at the top of the stalks (tassels) onto the female flowers (silks) of another kind of corn that is flowering at the same time.

- Make corn husk dolls to look like characters from the stories in this book.

- Make corn husk weavings such as mats to sit on while working in the garden.

- While you work on your gourd birdhouses, play and learn to recognize some recordings of the songs of birds that live in your area and that you would expect to nest in the birdhouses.

- Use your bottle gourd containers for garden tasks, such as for carrying seeds.

- Use different-size gourds to carve spoons and ladles.

- Read the Lacandon Maya story "The Farmer Who Wanted to Be a Jaguar" and create some of the animals in this story as scarecrow animals in your garden.

- Create a grasshopper scarecrow to watch over your garden.

- Read the children's book *Blue Potatoes, Orange Tomatoes* by Rosalind Creasy (San Francisco: Sierra Club Books, 1994).

- For books and magazines on organic gardening, write or call Rodale Press, 33 East Minor Street, Emmaus, PA 18049; (215) 967-5171.

# Chapter 5

# Native Harvests, Meals and Recipes

## Sharing the Corn
### *(Arikara—Plains)*

There was a time when the people of the plains did not have corn. One day, a young man went hunting. This young man had never been lucky and the people of his village considered him useless. So he was called Does Nothing. Yet Does Nothing hoped that he might do something good for his people.

That day, he searched for game for a long time without success. At last, he climbed a high hill and looked down into a valley. There, standing on the flat land between two rivers, stood a bull buffalo facing in the direction of the Winter Land. Does Nothing saw there was no way he could get close enough to that buffalo to shoot it with an arrow. The buffalo would see him coming. So he watched, waiting until the buffalo moved close enough to the trees where he could creep up on it. But the buffalo did not move. When dark came, the young man went home.

When Does Nothing came back the next day, he was surprised to look down from that hill and see the buffalo still standing in the same place. Now, though, it was facing the Sunrise Direction. All day the young hunter waited for the buffalo to move. How could an animal stand for so long without moving to eat or drink, without lying down to rest? Once again, though, it remained in that same spot until the sun set, and Does Nothing could see it no longer.

This was such a strange thing that the young man came back the next day. The buffalo was still there. Now it faced the direction of the Summer Land. Just as before, it stood all day without moving until it grew so dark that it could no longer be seen. It stood so still that Does Nothing felt certain it would not move even if he came down from his hilltop toward it. Yet something inside himself told him to watch and wait.

*They saw the many buffalo tracks and the strange plant growing from the mound of earth.*

On the fourth day, when Does Nothing returned to his hilltop, he saw that the buffalo bull now faced the Sunset Direction. Surely, some great mysterious power was at work. For that fourth day it stood without moving from dawn until dark. When Does Nothing returned home that night, he was so excited he could not sleep.

"Tomorrow," he said to himself, "I will go down and see why that buffalo has stood so long without moving."

Before the sun had risen, Does Nothing left the lodge and went to the hilltop. The light of the new day spread over the beautiful land, but the buffalo bull was gone. Does Nothing ran down the hill and crossed the river. The soft, moist earth of the flat plain was covered with buffalo tracks. They went from north to east, from east to south, from south to west and from west to north, making a great circle. There, in the center of the circle, was the place the great buffalo bull had stood. Only one single deep hoofprint was there, in the middle of a mound of earth. From the center of that footprint grew a strange plant.

Does Nothing looked closely at that plant. It was straight and green with wide straight leaves. He had never seen anything like it before. He hurried back to his village to tell the chiefs and the elders what he had found. The chiefs and the elders returned with him to that place. They saw the many buffalo tracks and the strange plant growing from the mound of earth.

"Surely," said the wisest of the elders, "this is a gift from Wakanda, the Great Mystery."

Just as the elder said that, the plant began to grow. It grew taller and taller. A single flower grew on top of it and then a new growth began to appear on the side of the plant. At the top of that new growth were pale yellow strands like hair. The people watched, not daring to come closer or touch the plant. Slowly the growth on the side of the plant changed color, turning from green to light brown.

"It seems," said another of the elders, "that this must be the fruit of the new plant and it has now ripened."

Still, no one dared to touch the plant.

Then Does Nothing stepped forward.

"My people," he said, "from my childhood I have done nothing useful. So it would be no loss to anyone if something bad should happen to me. I will see if this plant is meant to be a gift for the people."

Does Nothing gently placed his hand on the sides of the plant and then brought his hands down to the Earth.

"Wakanda," he said, "if this plant is a gift to us, I thank you for this blessing."

Then he picked the fruit and stripped back the husk. Within the husk was a stalk covered with many red grains. He plucked free a few of those grains and tasted them.

Everyone watched and waited. Then Does Nothing smiled.

"These are sweet to the taste as milk," he said. "Truly, this is a gift. It is a new food for the people."

Now other fruits had appeared on the plant. As they ripened, the people picked them. Some of those ears of corn had red kernels. Some were white, while others were yellow or blue.

"These must be seeds," the elders said. "We must not eat them all, but save some to plant in the spring."

The people did as the elders said. They let those kernels dry and then saved them over the winter. When the next spring came, they returned to that place between the rivers. There they made mounds of earth like the one in which the first mother cornstalk had grown. In each mound they planted four kernels of corn, one of each color—one for each of the four directions.

That field of corn did not grow as quickly as the first cornstalk had grown, but it grew tall throughout the summer. Ears formed on the tall cornstalks and when those ears turned brown in the late summer, the people made their first harvest. As they gathered that harvest, they spoke words of thanks to Wakanda. They spoke words thanking the bull buffalo who brought the corn. They spoke words of thanks to the Mother Corn herself. There was more than enough corn to feed all of the people throughout the winter.

Does Nothing saw this. "My People," Does Nothing said, "we must share this gift with the other peoples of the plains."

Everyone agreed. An invitation was sent out to all of the peoples around them. All were invited to come and share in the harvest. Six other nations came, among them the Omaha.

They all ate together and when they left, each of those nations took kernels of corn with them so that they could grow fields of their own.

That is how the young man who had done nothing before finally did something great. That is how the Mother Corn came to the plains and was shared by all the people.

🐾    🐾    🐾    🐾

## Bridges: From Legends to Life

The Arikara are a Native people of the Plains. The story of "Sharing the Corn" tells us that buffalo hunting is not the only traditional way of getting food among Plains peoples. Gardening is an important Plains tradition.

The young man named Does Nothing will not give up trying to do something good for his people. Does Nothing is determined and patient. He climbs to a high hill and, as he watches for several days, he sees a bull buffalo face in each of the Four Directions. The corn that comes as a gift from Wakanda, the Great Mystery, has four colors of kernels: red, white, yellow and blue. The Arikara plant four corn seeds, one of each color, in every mound of corn in their gardens.

The number four appears in many Native North American cultures. The *"Three Sisters Garden"* activity in Chapter 4 describes how some traditional Native gardeners plant corn, bean and squash seeds in the pattern of the Four Directions. Many cultures offer thanks to the Four Directions to show their gratitude for the gifts that help them live in the great Circle of Life. As the Arikara tell us in "Sharing the Corn," sharing and celebrating are also a part of being grateful.

There is another lesson to be learned from the Lacandon Maya story "The Farmer Who Wanted to Be a Jaguar," which appears earlier in the book. In this story the farmer Nuxi Balam's crops are being eaten by the animals of the rainforest. Nuxi's prayers are answered when he is turned into a jaguar who can drive the animals away. Then, all the animals start looking like people to him, and the human beings begin to resemble animals. Nuxi allows the "people" he sees through the eyes of a jaguar to come into his garden to eat, but he drives the "animals" away. A Mayan child hearing this story learns that it is folly to try to keep all the animals away from the harvest. That child also learns that we are all related—that animals also need to survive and that the garden needs to be shared with other forms of life.

### Food in Native North American Cultures

To Native North Americans food is not just something to eat. Throughout the year there are many celebrations and ceremonies that honor the importance of food in the Circle of Life. Many cultures, such as the Zuni, traditionally use corn of particular colors in their ceremonies. Certain colors stand for each of the Four Directions. Among the Zuni the colors of yellow, blue, red and white represent the directions of north, west, south and east, respectively.

Corn is a symbol of fertility in many Native cultures. This is why food is a part of many marriage practices and ceremonies. Traditionally, in the Southwest a young Hopi woman gives corn cakes to a young man during the February Bean Dance to show that she likes him. If a young Hopi woman decides whom she wants to marry, she makes a kind of blue cornbread wafer called a *piki*. Then, traveling along with her mother and maternal uncle, she leaves it on her chosen one's doorstep.[1] All the young man and his family must do to accept her marriage proposal is take the piki into their home. If they leave the bread there, the girl's family comes to gather it and she must look for another potential husband. Among the traditional Abenaki of the Eastern Woodlands, a young man's parents might make a marriage proposal for him by offering to the girl's mother a gift of a game animal he caught. This shows that the young man will be a good provider. The young woman accepts the marriage proposal by placing an ear of corn inside the young man's wigwam.

Food is also used widely as a gift between Native peoples and is the center of many celebrations. The ceremonies of the Kanienkahageh (Mohawk) people of the East, for example, include the Maple Syrup Ceremony (late spring), Strawberry Ceremony (early summer), Planting Ceremony (early summer), Bean Dance (midsummer), Green Corn Dance (midsummer) and Harvest Dance (end of summer).[2]

## Contributions of the Native Diet

Sit down for a meal in any part of North America today and you will find that most of the foods are from Native Americans. It is true that some important foods have been introduced to North America from Africa, Asia and Europe, such as wheat, oats, cabbage, apples, turnips, rice, citrus and most farm animals. But we eat many more Native American foods today than foods from any other continent.[3] Consider these Native foods and meals:

- corn: grits, popcorn, hominy, chips, bread, corn-on-the-cob, stew, meal, succotash, tortilla, Johnnycake, hush puppy, pone, syrup, nachos

- potato: chips, baked, french fries, mashed

- sweet potato

- tomato: sauce, salsa, juice

- squash: zucchini, pumpkin, hubbard, acorn, crookneck, cushaw

- bean: kidney, butter, snap, string, lima, tepary, common, navy, pole, Mexican frijole

- cassava or manioc: tapioca

- berry (forty-seven kinds of Native berries have been identified): blueberry (twenty varieties), elderberry (four varieties), gooseberry (more than a dozen varieties), wild grapes, ground cherries, wild currants, sour chokecherries, blackberries, manzanita, lemonadeberry (squawberry)

- avocado: guacamole

Many of the meals that we think of as modern are actually made of traditional Native foods. Cajun cooking is based on Native red beans and gumbo filé, a spice that comes from the sassafras tree. The Taino people of the Caribbean first came up with the idea of the barbecue—cooking meat and fish outdoors using a special sauce.[4] Jerky (dried meat sticks) and trail mix, containing dried fruit, are also Native inventions. The only domesticated animals native to North America, however, are the turkey, duck and dog.

Recipes found in countries throughout the world rely on foods from Native America. Imagine Italian cooking without tomato sauce, peppers or zucchini, an Irish diet lacking potatoes, or dishes from India without peanuts, cashews, cayenne and other hot peppers including chile. Parisian dessert trays would never be the same without "chocolat" or "French" vanilla. Green and kidney beans, Jerusalem artichoke, paprika, cranberry, pineapple, banana, papaya and guava are all native to the Americas and used widely overseas.

## Uses of the Three Sisters Crops

Native North Americans use corn, beans, squash and sunflowers in many imaginative ways, ranging from drinks to breads and from soups to roasted seeds. Many meals combine several kinds of crops. The Tohono O'odham (Papago) make a flour of corn, seeds and beans by grinding these crops just before eating them. Grinding is done with a stone called a *metate*. A *mano*, a handheld stone, is used to work the seeds or grains against the metate. The main part of any traditional O'odham meal is gruel or bread and a vegetable. Quechan (Yuman) cooks traditionally prepare corn, pumpkins, squash and beans in ceramic pots over a fire of mesquite wood. Most cultures make some form of traditional *succotash,* in which corn and beans are cooked, often along with sunflower seeds and other crops and seasonings.

CORN. Parched corn kernels are eaten that provide long-lasting energy. Corn silk is steamed or simmered to create a tea, and the dried kernels are freshly ground to make corn flour. Ears of corn are often roasted whole in the coals of a fire. Much of the corn from any harvest is dried on the cob and saved for eating at a later time. There are many kinds of corn that are extremely beautiful. The Tewa of New Mexico grow six colors of corn, and the Hopi have at least twenty different corn varieties.

BEANS. Beans are usually combined with other foods to make a meal. *Ga-na-tsi,* a favorite Cherokee soup, is made from beans,

# Pueblo Corn Grinding Song

I o ho ho, wai ai til an ni,

I o ho wai ai til an ni,

Tzi wa sho i ya ni i! He ye ye!

Yu weh pu ni a No e No li Na

Yu weh ha ni a No e No li Na

Tzi wa sho i ya ni i!

He ye ye He ye ye!

I o o ho wai ti kan na,

I o o ho wai ti lan ni,

Tzi wa sho i ya ni ni i!

He ye He ye ye He ye!

corn and hickory nuts. Boiled beans and bean bread are made by a number of cultures. Refried beans are popular in the Southwest. Varieties of dried beans are used for most meals, such as kidney, lima, butter, tepary, navy, common and black beans.

SQUASH. There are many kinds of squash, including acorn squash, summer crookneck and pumpkin. Traditional varieties may also include turban squash, hubbard and bush scallop. Butternut squash is a modern hybrid. Squash is often sliced up fresh and cooked in soups and casseroles. Dried squash and pumpkin flowers are ground to make an excellent seasoning. Fresh blossoms are mashed and used to thicken soups and other dishes. In the Eastern Woodlands, maple syrup is often added to sweeten baked and boiled squash and pumpkin. Traditionally throughout North America, squash and pumpkin were cut into strips and dried so that they could be preserved and eaten during the winter months. The seeds are often roasted until brown. Pumpkin seeds make a tasty, nutritious, high-energy trail food.

SUNFLOWERS. Sunflower seeds are eaten raw or baked. The seeds can be ground into a nut butter or added to other dishes. Mixtures of sunflower seeds, dried berries and grains are used for trail food.

MELONS. Although they have been widely adopted by many Native North American gardeners, melons were introduced by Europeans as long ago as 1494.[5] Native-grown melons are smaller than the familiar modern watermelon, but they are sweet and juicy. Melon is often eaten fresh.

Certain kinds can be cut into strips, dried and stored as winter food. Melon juice is boiled down to make a sweet syrup. Like the seeds of squash and pumpkin, melon seeds are sometimes roasted. The Quechan people boil melon seeds and grind them to make a gruel.

*Which is your favorite kind of squash?*

### Native Foods in Diet and Health

For thousands of years the Native peoples of North America have eaten the foods that grow naturally all around them. Their bodies have become adapted to local foods—they need these nutritional foods in order to stay healthy. Many Native Americans become ill when they eat foods that their systems are not used to.

The main foods of the traditional diet of the O'odham peoples of the Southwest—the Pima and the Papago—are the tepary bean, amaranth, sixty-day corn and a rich variety of Native wild plants including the mesquite pod and the acorn. Amaranth has one of the most balanced proteins found among plant foods. These Native foods help prevent diabetes by lowering the levels of insulin production and blood sugar after meals. After World War II the Pima and Papago switched to a modern American diet of fat, sugar and processed foods. Now they have some of the highest rates of diabetes in the world.[6] Diabetes affects about half of all Pima people who are thirty-five years or older—a higher rate than anyplace in the world.

When some of the O'odham stopped eating refined sugars, flours and fats, and once again began eating their traditional diet, they began to recover. Some people who were obese dropped 100 pounds (45 kilograms) or more. Research shows that tepary beans help moderate blood-sugar levels and control blood-glucose responses, both of which are causes of adult-onset diabetes.[7]

Corn syrup, a Native food, has a sugar more similar to that of human glucose than any other food that comes from plants. Although corn syrup is not good for diabetics, this kind of sweetener is easily digested by most people and does not tend to cause as many health problems as refined sugar.

### Food, Health and the Circle of Life

Food affects the health of people from every culture. Research by the U.S. Surgeon General shows that 68 percent of disease in the United States is related to diet. Thirty percent of all cancer is linked to what we eat, according to the National Academy of Sciences.[8] Clearly, whatever we put into the Circle of Life affects what we receive from it.

Corn and beans, when combined, are another example of the traditional value of Native foods. Many Native foods found

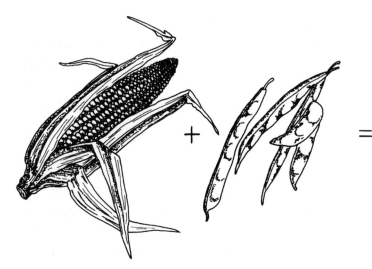

*Eat corn and beans to-gether for a source of pro-tein equal to a piece of meat.*

throughout the world complement one another—they provide high-quality protein when eaten together.[9] Nutritionists reported in the early 1970s that the combination of corn and beans, as well as of most legumes and grains, is a source of protein as complete as that found in a cut of meat.[10]

North Americans eat 50 to 100 percent more protein than our bodies need. Whenever an animal eats grain or any other plant to produce meat, about 90 percent of the food energy from the grain is used up by the animal. As a result, when human beings get protein directly from plant foods instead of from animals, there is more energy to go around—more people can be fed. A diet lower on the food chain is also more healthy; it lessens the risk of contracting certain cancers, coronary heart disease, high blood cholesterol, arteriosclerosis (hardening of the arteries), osteoporosis and strokes.

It is possible for most adults to get the protein they need for normal growth and maintenance directly from plant food. There are only three diets based on plant foods that cannot supply all the protein a healthy adult needs: those heavy in fruit, certain tubers (such as sweet potatoes or cassava) and junk food such as candy, chips and other foods made using refined flours, sugars and fat.[11] In her book *Diet for a Small Planet,* Frances Moore Lappé points out that babies, young children and nursing or pregnant women have greater protein needs than most people. Infants and young children cannot digest some plant foods as well as adults can, so it is important to take care that young people get enough protein in their diets. A good book for parents who want to help children eat more garden foods in their diet is *The Complete Guide and Cookbook for Raising Your Child as a Vegetarian* by Michael and Nina Shandler (New York: Schocken Books, 1981). This book also presents nutritional tips for pregnant women.

On the subject of eating plants and/or animals, it is important to remember that many cultures eat a particular diet as part of their cultural identity and way of life. We need to respect the diet that is chosen by every person and every culture. We all must eat to live. Our choice of diet is one of life's basic decisions that all human beings must make. When there are many choices because of plentiful food supplies, the decision can become a dilemma. For many peoples, however, there are few or no choices.

# Activities

## Native Meals

**ACTIVITY:** Prepare meals from recipes using plant foods native to North America and authentic traditional recipes from Native North American cultures.

**MATERIALS:** Specific food ingredients, kitchen utensils and equipment needed to prepare the Native plant dishes chosen from the recipes given here.

**DIGGING IN:**

The recipes in this activity are arranged by the kind of foods that are included in the recipe and/or the kind of meal that the recipe prepares. Groups of recipes appear in this order:

- corn recipes

- bean recipes

- squash and pumpkin recipes

- combination recipes (bean and corn recipes that are high in protein)

- snack, drink and dessert recipes

**1.** To refresh your memory, reread the last two parts of the "Bridges: From Legends to Life" section: "Native Foods in Diet and Health" and "Food, Health and the Circle of Life."

**2.** Look over the recipes that follow. Choose a simple recipe to start with, such as Quechan (Yuman) Squash.

**3.** Prepare more challenging meals as you start to feel comfortable with following recipes. Some of these recipes are very specific in the amounts and directions they give, while some are more general. It is not traditional to measure ingredients in cups and tablespoons! It is, therefore, important to keep a close eye on the meals you pre-

pare as they are cooking to make sure they come out just right. Do not be discouraged if what you cook is not exactly what you hoped for on the first try. Practicing and learning from experience are important parts of learning how to cook.

**4.** Do not be afraid to experiment and try new combinations of ingredients and ways of preparing recipes. Preparing food is part of the Circle of Life. It is fun—a living, growing, changing way of using your creative ideas and skills.

**5.** Enjoy these Native meals! We have found these simple, whole foods to be delicious.

### Recipe Notes

- Whenever a recipe calls for "oil" or "vegetable oil," we recommend that you use Native corn oil or sunflower oil. *Be careful: hot oil causes severe burns.*

- Grinding corn, seeds and other dry foods can be done with a grinding stone, mortar and pestle, blender or food processor.

- Dried corn kernels can be hard to find unless you grow and make your own. You can substitute fresh, canned or frozen corn, if necessary, but you will need to use a bit less water in the recipe to compensate for the additional moisture found in this corn.

- Some recipes call for a "nut butter." You can make a sunflower seed butter by grinding roasted sunflower seeds with a blender, grinding stone or mortar and pestle.

- Whenever these recipes call for beans, they refer to traditional varieties of dried beans, such as kidney, butter, brown, lima, tepary, common, navy and Mexican frijole beans. The recipes do not call for beans that are usually eaten fresh, such as string beans and snap beans.

### ENGLISH AND METRIC EQUIVALENTS
### FOR RECIPE MEASUREMENTS

For metric equivalents, you will need to calculate the fractions of these whole numbers as required for the quantities needed in each recipe.

1/2 teaspoon = 2.5 milliliters
1 teaspoon = 1/3 tablespoon = 5 milliliters
1 tablespoon = 3 teaspoons = 15 milliliters
1 cup = 16 tablespoons = 237 milliliters = 23.7 centiliters
1 pint = 2 cups = .47 liter (approximately 1/2 liter)
1 quart = 4 cups = 2 pints = .95 liter (approximately 1 liter)
1 pound = 16 ounces = 454 grams = .45 kilogram

### DRIED CORN AND BEANS

Some recipes call for dried corn and dried beans. You can use the corn and beans from your garden if you prepare them correctly. Make sure you are using the varieties of beans that are traditionally dried, such as those listed under "Beans" in the "Bridges: From Legends to Life" section of this chapter.

*A rainbow harvest of Hopi corn.*

## Drying Corn

This is the easiest way to dry corn:

1. Peel back the husks but be careful to leave them attached to the base of each ear of corn.
2. Braid or tie the husks together to make long ropes of corn.
3. Hang these ropes of corn in a *clean, sunny, dry, well-ventilated* place, away from where squirrels, mice, birds or raccoons might get them. Do not hang them in a basement or other dark, damp spot.
4. Leave the corn hanging until the kernels are thoroughly dried and hard to the touch. The kernels will shrivel up. The amount of time this will take depends on the temperature and moisture of your local climate and the kind of space you are using for drying. The drying will take at least four to six weeks.

## Drying Beans

1. Allow the beans to dry for a few weeks while they sit in their shells on the vine.
2. Remove the beans from the shells and place them on flat pans or dishes. Cover them with a clean cloth.
3. Keep the beans in a warm, dry place and allow them to continue drying.
4. Stir the beans daily for about two weeks.
5. When they are dry and hard to the touch, store the beans in clean, clear glass jars. Seal the jars airtight, and store them in a cool, dry, well-ventilated room. Be certain to label each jar with the variety of bean and the date the seeds were preserved.

### PARCHED CORNMEAL (NOKEHICK) AND KERNELS

Some recipes require parched cornmeal (*nokehick* or *noohkik*) or parched corn kernels. Parching corn softens and dries out the starches and gluten, making the corn easier to digest. This method can be used to parch other grains as well, such as sunflower seeds.

## Parching Cornmeal and Corn Kernels

1. Put dried cornmeal or kernels in a dry frying pan over low to medium heat. Do not use oil. You can also use a hot electric skillet set to "pancakes."
2. Stir the meal or kernels until they are lightly browned.

## Corn Recipes

### PLAINS CORNBREAD

1 pint cornmeal               salt (optional)
cold water

1. Pour the cornmeal into a large bowl. Add a little salt if you like.
2. Slowly add cold water to the cornmeal and stir it.
3. Work the cornmeal with your hands to make a stiff dough.
4. Roll and pat the dough into long thin "pones" (small ovals).
5. Bake slowly in a hot cast-iron skillet or wrapped in foil over hot coals. You can also bake the bread in an oven at 325°F (163°C). The bread is done when the outside turns a light brown.

**Note:** The traditional Southwestern "Kneeldown Bread" can be made as a variation on this recipe. In place of cornmeal and water, use fresh corn sliced from the cob. Mash the corn into mush and add a bit of salt if desired. Form the corn mush into cakes about 3 inches (7.5 centimeters) long, 2 inches (5 centimeters) wide and 1 inch (2.5 centimeters) thick. Steep the corn husks in hot water until they are flexible. Wrap the corn cakes in the corn husks and bake at low heat. This bread is traditionally made in a coal-filled fire pit.

### COAL-ROASTED CORN

Fresh ears of corn               seawater (1 cup of warm
                                 water with 1/2 teaspoon
                                 of salt  dissolved in it)

1. Pull the corn husks halfway down the ears of corn and take out the silk.
2. Sprinkle the exposed ear of corn with a little water.
3. Pull the husk back over the ear and twist shut.
4. Place the ear of corn over hot coals and turn it every few minutes. Make sure that all sides get exposed to the coals as you turn the corn. Allow it to cook for about 12 minutes. The husks will blacken along the edges, but the corn will be just right, with a pleasant barbecue flavor.

### CORN CHOWDER

3 cups dried corn kernels*      2 tablespoons nut butter
6 cups water                    1/2 pound sliced fresh
1 large or 2 small potatoes,       mushrooms
   diced                        1 tablespoon fresh dillweed
1 chopped onion                 garnish: seasonal herbs
1 chopped green pepper

1. Soak the corn in water overnight in a large, covered kettle.
2. Bring the corn to a boil then simmer it for 15 minutes.
3. Add all the remaining ingredients, except the mushrooms and dillweed, and simmer for 30 minutes.
4. Add the mushrooms and simmer for another 5 minutes.
5. Garnish and serve hot.

*For frozen corn, use three, 10-ounce (283 gm) boxes, add enough water to cover and omit step 1. Use a similar procedure for canned corn (3 cans) and go directly to step 2.

## JOHNNYCAKES*

| | |
|---|---|
| 1 cup stoneground white cornmeal† (any cornmeal will work) pinch of salt | 2 cups boiling water 2 tablespoons maple syrup 3/4 cup light or medium cream 1/4 cup corn oil for frying |

1. Mix the cornmeal and salt together well.
2. Scald this dry mixture with boiling water. Gradually add the water to the cornmeal as you stir rapidly. Add 1/2 cup of water at a time and work out the lumps. Stir well to create a smooth batter.
3. Stir in the maple syrup. Add more maple syrup if you like sweeter Johnnycakes.
4. Cool the cornmeal a little and thin the batter with cream until it is of medium consistency, not runny. Firm batter creates thicker Johnnycakes. Thinner batter forms pancake-like cakes.
5. Drop the batter by heaping a tablespoonful onto a medium-hot, well-oiled griddle. The cakes will spread out as they heat up.
6. Flip the Johnny-cakes after 6 minutes and cook another 5 minutes.

Johnnycakes can be eaten as crackers and with soups. You can also make them larger than is suggested here and eat them with butter and maple syrup like small pancakes. This recipe makes about 12 to 18 Johnny-cakes.

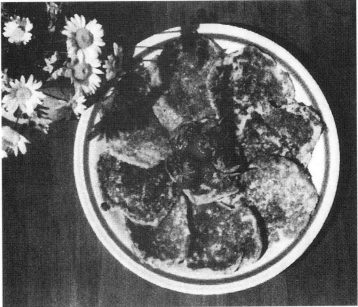

*Johnnycakes.*

*This traditional recipe is courtesy of Dr. Ella W. T. Sekatau of the Narragansett Indian Nation.

†You can obtain white cornmeal by mail order from the Kenyon Corn Meal mill, located on the traditional lands of the Narragansett Indian Nation. The Narragansett's tribal offices are just miles away. Write or call: Kenyon Corn Meal, P.O. Box 221, West Kingston, RI 02892; (800) 753-6966.

## HOMINY GRITS

| | |
|---|---|
| 5 cups water | 1 tablespoon nut butter |
| 1 cup hominy grits | 1 tablespoon honey |

1. Boil the water in a saucepan.
2. Pour in the grits gradually while you stir.
3. Stir in the nut butter and honey.
4. Cover and cook for 20 minutes or until all the water is absorbed.

The grits can be sweetened, or you can add herb spices. Grits have many uses: they make a good breakfast cereal, soup and dinner.

## TORTILLAS

| | |
|---|---|
| 2 cups corn flour (*masa harina*) | 1/2 teaspoon salt (optional) |
| 1-1/3 cups lukewarm water | |

1. Put the corn flour in a bowl. Stir in the salt, if desired. Stir in 1 cup of water.
2. Work this mixture thoroughly with your hands for about 10 minutes to form a soft dough. Add a bit more water, if necessary. Do not make the dough too wet or it will stick to the griddle. Corn flour, which is also called *masa harina,* is actually a finely ground cornmeal that is available in specialty food shops. It will not form the kind of sticky dough that you are used to, but will retain a grainy feel.
3. Divide the dough and form into egg-sized balls.
4. Between sheets of wax paper, roll out each ball, one at a time, into 4-inch (10-centimeter) flat circles.
5. Peel off the top piece of wax paper and put the tortilla into the palm of your hand with the remaining wax paper side up.
6. Peel off the remaining paper and carefully put the tortilla on a medium-hot, *ungreased* griddle. This process is tricky and will take some practice because the cakes tend to fall apart. The action of transferring the tortilla to the griddle must be done swiftly and gently with care not to break the cake into pieces. The cakes will release more easily if your hand is coated in dry

corn flour. As soon as each cake touches the griddle, it forms a solid, sturdy tortilla. You will need to replace the wax paper occasionally when it becomes too damp, because the cakes will begin to stick.

7. Cook until the edges curl—about 1 minute—then flip with a spatula.
8. Cook 1 minute more until the tortilla is golden brown.

*Tortillas.*

## Bean Recipes

### BOILED BEANS

2 cups dried beans          cold water
pinch of salt

1. Pour the beans into a large saucepan. Add cold water to about 1 inch above the top of the beans.
2. Cover and allow to soak overnight.
3. By morning the beans will have absorbed most of the water. Add more water and a pinch of salt. Boil the beans until they are tender. Add more water if necessary while boiling.

## REFRIED BEANS
### (Traditional Southwestern)

Boiled beans                    water (if necessary)
  (see preceding recipe)    3 tablespoons corn oil

1. Drain off the water and mash the boiled beans to a paste. Add a bit more water if the beans are too dry to form a thick paste.
2. Fry the bean paste in an oiled skillet.

## BEAN BREAD
### (Oklahoma Cherokee)
### (corn and bean protein combination)

1 cup pinto or chili beans      1 cup cornmeal
1 teaspoon salt                 water
seasoning of your choice        3 tablespoons corn oil

1. Soak the beans over night as described in the recipe for Boiled Beans.
2. Cover the beans with more water. Cook the beans with the salt and seasonings for about 2 hours or until tender. Add extra water to create a broth as the beans cook.
3. Drain off the bean broth into a measuring cup and add enough water to make a total of 3 cups of broth/water. Bring this to a boil in a saucepan.
4. Stir 1 cup of cornmeal into the broth/water.
5. Cook the cornmeal for about 15 minutes. Stir constantly. Let the water boil away until the cornmeal is very thick.
6. Let the cornmeal and beans cool thoroughly.
7. Preheat the oven to 350°F (177°C).
8. Mash the beans.
9. Mix the cornmeal well with the mashed beans, and shape with your hands into pones (small ovals about 4 to 5 inches [10 to 13 centimeters] long).
10. Bake on an oiled baking sheet for about 30 minutes or until golden brown.

## Squash and Pumpkin Recipes

### HOT COAL SQUASH

butternut or acorn squash          maple syrup

1. Cut a butternut or acorn squash in half and remove the seeds. Save the seeds for roasting (see the recipe for Roasted Pumpkin or Squash Seeds).
2. Wash, then wrap, the halves of the squash in aluminum foil.
3. Bury the squash completely in the hot coals of a fire. Cook for about 20 minutes or until it is tender and a fork slides in easily. As an alternative, you can bake the squash in a 325°F (163°C) oven for about 40 minutes.
4. Sweeten the squash with a little maple syrup.

### QUECHAN (YUMAN) SQUASH

squash for baking              pinch of salt
water

1. Clean and peel a fresh squash.
2. Cut the squash into small pieces.
3. Boil the squash until it is tender.
4. Drain and mash the squash.
5. Season it lightly with salt.

### YELLOW SQUASH SOUP

2 pounds or 2 medium          1 tablespoon sunflower seed oil
  winter squash or            1 quart water
  acorn squash                1 tablespoon fresh, chopped
2 scallions or wild leeks,        dillweed
  sliced (including tops)     garnish: toasted sunflower or
1 tablespoon honey              squash seeds

1. Pour the water into a large covered pot. Simmer the squash, scallions or leeks, honey and oil for about 30 minutes until the squash is tender. Allow it to cool a bit.
2. Mash the squash to a puree and add the dillweed.
3. Heat and simmer for 5 more minutes. Add more water if you want a thinner soup.
4. Garnish with seeds and serve hot or cold.

## TAOS PUMPKIN

| 4 ears of fresh sweet corn | 2 tablespoons corn oil |
| 2 small cooking pumpkins | 1/3 cup water |
| 1/2 onion | |

1. Cut the kernels off the ears of corn.
2. Cut the pumpkins and onion into fine cubes.
3. In a large frying pan, fry the corn, pumpkin and onion in corn oil.
4. Add the water, cover and steam until done.

## FRIED SQUASH BLOSSOMS

| 3/4 cup flour | 1 cup goat's milk |
| 1/2 teaspoon chili powder | (cow's milk will do) |
| pinch of salt | 3–4 cups corn oil |
| 1/4 teaspoon baking soda | 1 quart squash blossoms, washed, with stems removed |

1. Mix together the flour, salt, chili powder and baking soda.*
2. Stir the milk into the dry mixture to create a batter.
3. Fill a medium-sized frying pan with about 1-1/2 inches (4 centimeters) of corn oil. Heat the corn oil to between 325°F (163°C) and 350°F (177°C). (Test with a cooking thermometer.)
4. Cut each squash blossom into 2 or 3 pieces.
5. Dip the squash blossoms into the batter.
6. Carefully drop the batter-coated blossoms into the hot oil. Fry them until brown and crisp.
7. Drain the fried squash blossoms on paper towels and serve.

This recipe makes about one dozen fried squash blossoms.

*Baking soda is not in the traditional recipe. We added it to help the dough rise.

*This Taos woman is holding a large, pumpkin-like squash.*

## HAVASUPAI SQUASH-BLOSSOM CORN PUDDING

3 ears of green corn
5 cups water

2–3 cups squash blossoms
salt

1. Cut the green corn off the cobs.
2. Boil 4 cups of water, add the corn, cover and cook it over medium heat for about 30 minutes.
3. Wash the squash blossoms and pinch off the stems.
4. In another pot, boil the squash blossoms until tender (about 15 minutes), then drain off the water.
5. Mash the cooked blossoms to a pulp.
6. Add the blossom mash to the green corn and simmer until thick, about 1 hour.
7. Season to taste with salt.

## Combination Recipes

## PUEBLO SUCCOTASH
### (corn and bean protein combination)

1 cup chopped onion
2 chopped fresh tomatoes
1/2 cup sunflower seeds
1/2 teaspoon chili powder
    (optional)
water

1-1/2 cups cooked
    dried corn
1-1/2 cups cooked lima
    beans (see the recipe for
    Boiled Beans)

1. Combine all ingredients in a heavy saucepan. Add enough water to make a kind of vegetable stew.
2. Simmer over low heat for about 1 hour or until the flavors blend and all ingredients are cooked. Keep adding water as needed.
3. After everything is cooked, let the succotash sit for an hour or two. You can eat the succotash as soon as it is done, but it tastes even better after the flavors have mingled while it sits in the refrigerator for a few days.

## HIDATSA FOUR-VEGETABLES MIXED
### (corn and bean protein combination)

4 handfuls of beans
1 medium-sized winter
  squash
several cups of water

4 handfuls of parched
  sunflower seeds
6 handfuls of parched corn
  (see the directions for
  parching corn on page 125)

1. Put the beans in a saucepan and fill the pan with water to a few inches above the beans. Cover and soak the beans overnight.
2. Boil the beans until they are tender. Add more water as needed.
3. Cut the winter squash into chunks. Boil or steam the chunks in a separate saucepan until soft. Mash the squash.
4. Add the mashed squash to the beans and stir them together.
5. Grind up the sunflower seeds and corn. Add them to the squash and beans. Add water to give the mix the consistency of a stew.
6. Boil these ingredients for about a half hour to let the flavors blend. Add more water if necessary.

## Snack, Drink and Dessert Recipes

## INDIAN PUDDING

This is a modern adaptation of a traditional recipe. We include it here because it is too delicious to leave out! This dessert is called "Indian Pudding" because it is made of "Indian" meal (corn) and not English meal (wheat, barley or rye).

1/4 cup cornmeal
1 teaspoon salt
1 cup cold water
2 cups scalded milk
1 well-beaten egg
1/4 cup brown sugar

1/2 cup molasses
1 tablespoon butter
1 teaspoon ground cinnamon
1/2 teaspoon ground ginger
1/4 teaspoon nutmeg
1 cup cream
raisins (optional)

1. Preheat the oven to 300°F (150°C).
2. Combine the cornmeal and salt and mix well. Add this to the cold water and stir thoroughly. Stir in 2 cups scalded milk.
3. Boil the mixture for 10 minutes, stirring constantly and gently.

4. Combine the beaten egg, brown sugar, molasses, butter and spices in a bowl and blend well.
5. Stir this mixture into the boiling cornmeal. Add a handful of raisins, if desired.
6. Pour the mixture into a buttered casserole that will hold at least 1-1/2 quarts. Bake it for 1/2 hour.
7. Stir in the cream.
8. Bake 2 hours more. Serve hot or cold. This pudding is excellent when served hot with vanilla ice cream on top.

## ROASTED PUMPKIN OR SQUASH SEEDS

| | |
|---|---|
| fresh pumpkin or squash seeds | corn oil salt |

*Indian Pudding.*

1. Dry the seeds on a tray in the sun or in a slightly warmed oven.
2. Preheat the oven to 250°F (120°C).
3. Put the seeds in a bowl and mix them well with just enough corn oil to coat them.
4. Add salt to taste and stir well.
5. Spread the seeds on an oiled baking sheet.
6. Roast them in the oven, stirring occasionally for about 20 minutes or until they start to turn brown.

## CORN DRINK
### (*Atol de Elote* or "Corn-on-the-Cob Gruel")
### (Mayan)

| | |
|---|---|
| 3 ears of fresh sweet corn | 2 teaspoons sugar |
| 3/4 teaspoon cinnamon | 3 cups water |

1. Cut the kernels off the ears of corn.
2. Put the corn kernels through a blender or food processor and mash well.
3. Add the cinnamon and sugar to the corn.
4. Put the spiced, sweetened corn in a saucepan with 3 cups of water.
5. Stir the entire mixture over medium heat and bring it to a boil for just a minute or two. Add a bit more water or spice if desired.
6. Serve hot.

# POPCORN

popcorn                          salt
corn oil

1. Pour just enough corn oil into a large saucepan to coat the bottom.
2. Drop two popcorn kernels into the oil and cover the pan.
3. Cook over medium heat until the kernels pop. *Be careful not to get the oil too hot. It should be smoking just a little when it is ready.*
4. Add enough popcorn to cover the bottom of the pan with a layer one kernel deep. Cover.
5. Continue to heat for a few minutes and shake occasionally as the kernels pop.
6. Turn the heat off when the popping slows down. Be careful not to cook for too long or the kernels will burn.
7. Pour into a bowl and add salt or other seasonings to taste.

# SUNFLOWER SEED CAKES

3 cups raw, shelled            6 tablespoons fine
  sunflower seeds,               cornmeal
  fresh or dried               2 teaspoons maple syrup
4 cups water                   1/2 cup sunflower oil

1. Simmer the sunflower seeds in water in a covered saucepan for about 1 hour.
2. Drain the seeds and grind them up in a blender or food processor.
3. Combine the cornmeal and maple syrup and mix well.
4. Stir the cornmeal and maple syrup into the ground sunflower seeds 1 tablespoon at a time. This is best done by working the mix with your hands into a stiff dough.
5. Shape the dough into firm, flat cakes about 3 inches (7.5 centimeters) in diameter.

6. Brown the cakes on a hot, oiled skillet over low heat with the cover on. Be sure to turn them over and brown both sides well. Cook about 6 minutes on the first side, then about 5 minutes after the cakes have been flipped.

7. Drain the cakes on brown paper. Serve hot. This recipe makes about 14 cakes.

## An International Garden Feast

**ACTIVITY:** Prepare a feast of garden dishes from cultures around the world.

**MATERIALS:** Cookbooks with recipes from around the world; copies of books with information and recipes for plant diets, such as those listed below and in the "Digging In" section; food ingredients as needed for recipes chosen; kitchen utensils and equipment as needed; plates, cups, silverware, etc. (not the disposable kind).

**DIGGING IN:**

**1.** Reread the information in the "Bridges: From Legends to Life" section that addresses the nutritional and cultural reasons for eating low on the food chain by eating garden foods. Focus on the discussion of protein in the diet, on our true need for protein and on the health benefits of eating less meat. Understand that healthy adults do not need animal food in their diet, but that babies, young children and pregnant or nursing mothers have special protein needs. Two good books for information and recipes on this topic are *Diet for a Small Planet* (twentieth anniversary edition) by Frances Moore Lappé (New York: Ballantine, 1991) and *The Complete Guide and Cookbook for Raising Your Child as a Vegetarian* by Michael and Nina Shandler (New York: Schocken Books, 1981).

**2.** Gather some cookbooks that contain recipes from many different cultures around the world, as well as some vegetarian cookbooks. Check the cookbook section of your local public library. Share these recipes and use them to plan an exciting international garden feast. Be sure to include some foods from the traditional meals of your own cultural background(s). Prepare a few simple dishes at first. Then, with some practice, you can follow the more difficult recipes. Include a well-rounded selection of foods from many different cultures and parts of the world. Enjoy!

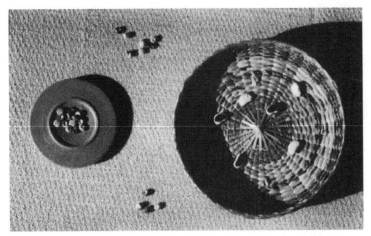

*Cherokee Butterbean Game.*

## Cherokee Butterbean Game

**ACTIVITY:** Play a traditional Cherokee game using butterbeans.

**MATERIALS:** Six butterbeans (six *large* lima beans can be substituted); twenty-four kernels of dried corn; basket, basket lid or other round, lightweight container at least 12 inches (30 centimeters) in diameter and 1-1/2 inches (4 centimeters) deep in which to toss the butterbeans; pot or bowl for the corn kernels; paper and pencil; felt-tip marking pen.

**DIGGING IN:** This is a variation on the traditional Cherokee Butterbean Game. It can be played by several individual players or several teams. Traditionally, this game uses three butterbeans that have been split in half. We do not recommend this because it is very easy to cut oneself while splitting a dried butterbean from edge to edge. We use six whole butterbeans (or six large lima beans). Color one side of each bean with the felt-tip marker.

To play a round of the Butterbean Game each player will:
**1.** Place the six butterbeans in the round basket, basket lid or other lightweight container.

**2.** Gently flip the butterbeans into the air and catch them in the basket.

**3.** Look at how the butterbeans have landed. Only three combinations are counted as a score:

- All butterbeans land with plain sides up: **6 points**

- All butterbeans land with marked sides up: **4 points**

- A single butterbean lands with one color facing up and the other five butterbeans land with the other color facing up: **2 points**

- Three butterbeans land with the same color facing up and the other three butterbeans land with the other color facing up: **1 point**

**4.** If the player scores during a turn, he or she will gather up the number of corn kernels from the pot that equals that score. The kernels will be kept in front of that player.

**5.** Players or teams take turns flipping the beans. Each flip that scores earns that player or team another turn. If the flip does not score, it becomes the next player's or team's turn.

**6.** The game is over when all the corn kernel counters have been removed from the pot. The team left with the highest score—the most corn counters—wins.

## Branching Out

- Reread the Tutelo story "The Bean Woman" in Chapter 4 and the Lacandon Maya story "The Farmer Who Wanted to Be a Jaguar." Prepare some recipes from this chapter and from other cookbooks that include the Native foods mentioned in these stories.

*A bounty of Native foods (clockwise from left of basket): tomatoes, chili peppers, potatoes and peanuts and (in basket from left to right) avocados and sweet potatoes.*

- Read Chapter 5 of *Keepers of the Night: Native American Stories and Nocturnal Activities for Children* (Golden, Colo.: Fulcrum, 1994). This chapter explains how to build a campfire with a bow drill and has more ideas for cooking Native foods and telling Native stories. It also shows how to make and play a number of Native games.

- In the Arikara story "Sharing the Corn," the people invited their neighbors to come and share the harvest. Prepare a meal of Native foods from the recipes in this chapter and invite some of your neighbors to share it with you.

- Does Nothing is a poor hunter in "Sharing the Corn." He tries hard, but is not successful. He discovers the gift of corn because he is determined to do something good for his people. Create your own story about someone who struggles, then finally succeeds because he or she does not give up.

- Reread "The Farmer Who Wanted to Be a Jaguar" to see what happens to someone who tries not to share his food with the animals. Search through the "Bridges: From Legends to Life" section and the activities in Chapter 4 to find some ways of sharing the garden with animals. Share some of your corn and other food with the animals each time you make a Native meal.

- Make a journal to keep track of your meals for a few days. Describe what you are eating and what part of the world those foods and recipes come from.

- Hold a potluck for which everyone prepares a meal made with a recipe and foods from their own cultural backgrounds.

- Write your own stories about foods from other continents. In the stories, explain how those foods came to be. Learn something about the people, plants and animals in these different places and include them in your stories.

- Gather your favorite recipes and make up your own international garden cookbook.

- Search for and play other Native North American games. The most comprehensive book available is *Games of the*

*North American Indians* by Stewart Culin (New York: Dover Publications, 1975).

- Read these books: *Earthmaker's Lodge: Native American Folklore, Activities and Foods,* edited by Barrie Kavasch (Peterborough, N. H.: Cobblestone Publishing, 1994); *Blue Corn and Chocolate* by Elisabeth Rozin (New York: Knopf, 1992); *A Native American Feast* by Lucille Recht Penner (New York: Macmillan, 1994); *Enduring Harvests: Native American Foods and Festivals for Every Season* by E. Barrie Kavasch (Old Saybrook, Conn.: Globe Pequot Press, 1995); and *New Native Cooking* by Dale Carson (New York: Random House, 1996).

# Notes

## Chapter 1

1. Gilbert L. Wilson. *Buffalo Bird Woman's Garden: Agriculture of the Hidatsa Indians*. St. Paul: Minnesota Historical Society Press, 1987, p. 27.
2. Frances G. Lombardi and Gerald Scott Lombardi. *Circle Without End*. Happy Camp, Calif.: Naturegraph Publishers, 1982, p. 25.
3. Gary Paul Nabhan. *Enduring Seeds: Native American Agriculture and Wild Plant Cultivation*. San Francisco: North Point Press, 1989, pp. 95–96.
4. Barrie Kavasch. *Native Harvests: Recipes and Botanicals of the American Indian*. New York: Vintage Books, p. xv.
5. Edward O. Wilson, "Threats to Biodiversity." *Scientific American,* vol. 261, no. 3 (September 1989), pp. 108–116.
6. Jack Weatherford. *Native Roots: How the Indians Enriched America*. New York: Crown, 1991, p. 128.
7. Nabhan, *Enduring Seeds,* pp. 52–53.
8. Kavasch, *Native Harvests,* p. xvi.
9. Boyce Rensberger, "Diminishing Diversity." *The Washington Post*. Reprinted in *Valley News* (May 18, 1992), pp. 15–18.
10. Gary Paul Nabhan. *Songbirds, Truffles, and Wolves: An American Naturalist in Italy*. New York: Penguin Books, 1993, p. 52.
11. See Chapter 14 in *Keepers of Life: Discovering Plants Through Native American Stories and Earth Activities for Children* by Michael J. Caduto and Joseph Bruchac (Golden, Colo.: Fulcrum, 1994), for extensive information and activities about threatened and endangered plants.

## Chapter 2

1. This list is adapted, with permission, from material produced by the Institute for American Indian Studies, 38 Curtis Road, P.O. Box 1260, Washington, CT 06793; (203) 868-0518, as found in *Native American Sourcebook: A Teacher's Resource on New England Native Peoples* by Barbara Robinson (Concord, Mass.: Concord Museum, 1988), p. 167. For ordering information, write or call Concord Museum, 200 Lexington Road, P.O. Box 146, Concord, MA 01742; (508) 369-9763. The Institute for American Indian Studies involves Native Americans in their programs, which teach about Native Americans, past and present, through exhibits, events, educational services, research projects and publications.

## Chapter 3

1. Eliot Coleman. *The New Organic Grower*. Chelsea, Vt.: Chelsea Green, 1989, pp. 43–44.
2. Marjorie Waters, *The Victory Garden Kids' Book: A Fun Guide to Growing Vegetables, Fruits and Flowers*. Old Saybrook, Conn.: Globe Pequot Press, 1994, p. 54.
3. Ibid., p. 53.

# Chapter 4

1. Jack Weatherford. *Native Roots: How the Indians Enriched America* New York: Crown, 1991, pp. 6–11.
2. Ibid., p. 11.
3. Ibid.
4. Ibid., p. 113.
5. Mary Pohl (ed.). *Prehistoric Lowland Maya Environment and Subsistence Economy.* Cambridge, Mass.: Harvard University Press, 1985, p. 14.
6. Peter Harrison (ed.). *Pre-Hispanic Mayan Agriculture.* Albuquerque: University of New Mexico Press, 1978, pp. 325–335.
7. Catherine Caufield. *In the Rainforest.* Chicago: University of Chicago Press, 1991, p. 125.
8. The story of the extermination of the bison in the late 1800s is told in detail in the "Discussion" section at the beginning of Chapter 17 in *Keepers of the Animals* by Michael J. Caduto and Joseph Bruchac. Golden, Colo.: Fulcrum, 1991.
9. Lynn Ceci. "Squanto and the Pilgrims: On Planting Corn 'In the Manner of the Indians.'" In James A. Clifton (ed.), *The Invented Indian: Cultural Fictions and Government Policies.* New Brunswick, N.J.: Transaction Publishing, 1990, pp. 71–89.
10. Nanepashemet. "Growing a Native Garden Based upon Southern New England Techniques." Unpublished manuscript and personal correspondence, 1995.
11. See Chapter 4 in both *Keepers of Life* and *Keepers of the Night* for information and activities revolving around Native moons and celebrations.
12. Harvey Arden and Steve Wall. *Wisdomkeepers: Meetings with Native American Spiritual Elders.* Hillsboro, Ore.: Beyond Words Publishing, 1990, pp. 118–119.
13. Jack Weatherford. *Indian Givers: How the Indians of the Americas Transformed the World.* New York: Fawcett Columbine, 1988, p. 83.
14. Ibid., p. 85.
15. Gary Paul Nabhan. *Enduring Seeds: Native American Agriculture and Wild Plant Cultivation.* San Francisco: North Point Press, 1989, pp. 36–37.
16. Ibid., pp. 72–73.
17. See Chapter 18 in *Keepers of the Earth* for the Hopi story "Kokopilau, The Hump-Backed Flute Player."
18. I (Michael Caduto) am very grateful to the late Nanepashemet of the Assonet Band of the Wampanoag Nation for his generosity in sharing the details on the traditional Wampanoag Three Sisters Garden. This information was invaluable as I field-tested these methods over the course of several years in my own garden.
19. Adapted with permission from *Buffalo Bird Woman's Garden*, as told to Gilbert L. Wilson. St. Paul: Minnesota Historical Society Press, 1987.

# Chapter 5

1. Carolyn Niethammer. *American Indian Food and Lore: 150 Authentic Recipes.* New York: Collier Books, 1974, p. xxvii.

2. Barbara (Kawenehe) Barnes, Mike (Kanentakeron) Mitchell and Joyce (Konwahwihon) Thompson, *Traditional Teachings*. Cornwall Island, Ont.: North American Indian Traveling College, 1984, p. 10.

3. Jack Weatherford. *Indian Givers: How the Indians of the Americas Transformed the World.* New York: Fawcett Columbine, 1988, pp. 99–115.

4. Ibid., p. 109.

5. Alfred W. Crosby, Jr. *The Columbian Exchange: Biological Consequences of 1492.* Westport, Conn.: Greenwood Press, 1972, pp. 67–68.

6. Kenny Ausubel. *Seeds of Change: The Living Treasure.* San Francisco: HarperSanFrancisco, 1994, p. 164.

7. Ibid., p. 165.

8. Ibid., p. 105.

9. Frances Moore Lappé. *Diet for a Small Planet* (twentieth anniversary edition). New York: Ballantine, 1991, p. 172.

10. Ibid., pp. 159–160, 402.

11. Ibid., p. 162.

# Glossary and Pronunciation Key to Native North American Words, Names and Cultures

**Abenaki** (Ab´eh-nah-kee or Ab´-er-nah-kēe). "Dawn Land People." A northeastern Algonquin group whose traditional homelands include present-day Vermont and New Hampshire.

**Akimel O'odham** (Ah-key´-mel Oh´-Oh-dum). {Pima} "River People." A people of the valleys of the Gila and Salt Rivers in Arizona. See *Pima*.

**Akinchob** (Ah-keen´-chop). {Maya} One of the deities of the Lacandon Maya people of the Mexican rainforest in Chiapas Province. Akinchob is the patron of the farmers.

**Aniyunwiya** (Ah-nee-yoon´-wi-yah). {Cherokee} "Real People." A Native people whose original homelands include the areas now known as Tennessee, Georgia, Kentucky and North Carolina. One of the so-called Five Civilized Tribes of the Southeast who adopted much of European material culture by the early 1800s.

**Apache** (Ah-pah´-chee). From the Zuni word *apachu,* meaning "enemy." The Apache call themselves *N´de* or *Tinde,* from *tinneh* (tih-ney´), meaning "The People." Their traditional homeland stretched from Kansas into Mexico and from Oklahoma into Arizona. They practiced some agriculture, growing corn and other crops, but relied much more heavily on hunting and gathering.

**Arikara** (Ah´-rih-kah-rah). A people whose traditional earth-lodge villages were in central South Dakota. Currently one of the Three Affiliated Tribes—Mandan, Hidatsa and Arikara—located in west-central North Dakota.

**Atsina** (At-see´-nah). Probably from the Blackfoot word meaning "Gut People." The Atsina are also known as the *Gros Ventre.* An Algonquian-speaking people of the plains whose traditional lands range from the Milk River branch of the Missouri River in northern Montana and north into southern Saskatchewan. They are closely related to the Arapahos, with whom they migrated west to this area in the 1700s from the Red River region of Minnesota and North Dakota. Many live today with the Assiniboine on the Fort Belknap Reservation in northern Montana. Recent years have seen a strengthening of Atsina cultural traditions and a revival of the ancestral language.

**Aztec** (Az´-tek). See *Nahua.*

**Blackfoot.** See *Siksika.*

**Buffalo Bird Woman.** See *Maxidiwiac.*

**Cahokia** (Kah-hoh´-kee-ya). A large ancient city that includes a complex of pyramids, temples and other monumental earthworks built more than one thousand years ago, close to the Mississippi River in what is now Illinois.

**Cherokee** (Chair´-oh-key). From *Tsa-la-gi* (chah´-lah-gee), derived from the **Choctaw** *chiluk-ki*, meaning "cave dwellers." See *Aniyunwiya*.

**Cheyenne** (Shy-ann´). Name commonly used for the people who call themselves *tsitsitsas* (seet-seet´-sahs), meaning the "Striped Arrow People." From the Lakota Sioux word *shalyena*, meaning "Those Who Speak Strangely." Formerly settled agriculturalists, the Cheyenne moved onto the plains and became nomadic buffalo hunters with the coming of the horse in the 1700s.

**chultun** (Chuhl´-toon). {Maya} An underground pit used for storing grain.

**copal** (Koh´-phal). A ceremonial incense made from the sap of a plant by the Lacandon Maya. From the Nahuatl word *copalli*, meaning "resin."

**Creek.** See *Muskogee*.

**Diné** (Dih-ney´). "The People." An Athabascan people related to the Apache. Their traditional homeland is the Four Corners area of the Southwest. The Diné or Navajo are the most numerous of the Native peoples of the United States. Formerly nomadic raiders, within the last century in their current homeland—parts of Arizona, New Mexico, and southern Utah—they have developed a lifestyle based on herding and agriculture.

**Eskimo** (Es´-kih-mo). Cree word meaning "Fish Eaters," applied to those arctic peoples who call themselves *Inuit*. See *Inuit*.

**Farmer, Chief Louis** {Onondaga}. 1915– . One of the traditional leaders chosen by the women of his clan to represent the Onondaga Nation of the Iroquois League.

**ga-na-tsi** (ga-naht´-see). {Cherokee} A soup made from corn, beans and hickory nuts.

**Gros Ventre** (Grohs Ven´-truh). See *Atsina*.

**Haudenosaunee** (Ho-de-no-show´-ne). "People of the Longhouse." The Haudenosaunee (Iroquois) are a confederation of Native nations. The five original Haudenosaunee nations were the Mohawk, the Oneida, the Onondaga, the Cayuga and the Seneca. (When their lands were taken from them by white settlers, the Tuscarora people migrated north from North Carolina and became the Sixth Nation.) Their confederacy was known as the Great League and was symbolized by a giant white pine tree, the Tree of Peace. The Haudenosaunee relied equally upon agriculture and hunting to feed their people.

**Havasupai** (Hah-vah-soo´-pi). "People of the Blue Creek." A Native people whose village, Supai, is located at the bottom of the Havasu Canyon, which leads into the Grand Canyon of the Colorado River in Arizona.

**Hidatsa** (Hee-daht´-sah). The Hidatsa people of North Dakota were called, along with the Mandan, the "farmers, merchants and bankers of the plains" until they were decimated by smallpox in the early 1800s.

Currently part of the Three Affiliated Tribes of Fort Berthold, North Dakota.

**Hohokam** (Ho´-ho-kem). From a Pima word meaning "Ancient Ones." The name is applied to certain of the "vanished" ancient peoples of Arizona who used irrigation ditches and built extensive villages.

**Hopi** (Ho´-pee). "Peaceful Ones." One of the Pueblo peoples, the Hopi live in the high plateau country of northeastern Arizona, where they are extremely sophisticated dryland farmers.

**Huron** (Hyu´-ron). A Native people of the St. Lawrence Valley and Ontario region of Canada who call themselves *Wyandot*. Their name is drawn from the French *hure*, meaning "disheveled head of hair."

**Inca** (In´-kah). {Quechua} Name applied to a confederacy of Quechua-speaking Andean peoples of South America whose vast territory included parts of present-day Peru and Bolivia. Certain crops of the Quechuan peoples, such as the potato, are now used all over the world. The literal meaning of *Inca* in Quechuan is "prince" or "male of royal blood," and the word was used to refer to the leaders of the Incaic Empire.

**Inuit** (In´you-it). "Real People." The word *Inupiaq* is used in Alaska and western Canada. A people of the Far North who rely upon hunting and fishing and their ingenuity to survive in the Arctic. See *Eskimo*.

**Iroquois** (Ear´-oh-kwah or Ear-oh-kwoy´). From the Algonquin word *ireohkwa*, meaning "real snakes." See *Haudenosaunee*.

**kachina** (kah-chee´-nah). {Hopi} Powerful beings who exist much of the year as clouds, but take physical form at certain times in the shape of masked dancers whose coming is related to the return of the rain. Small wooden kachina dolls (which have become collectors' items) are used to help teach Hopi children about the many different kachinas.

**Kanienkahageh** (Gah-nee-yen-gah-hah´-gey). "People of the Land of the Flint." One of the five original Haudenosaunee nations. See *Haudenosaunee* and *Mohawk*.

**Kokopilau** (Ko-ko-pee´-le). {Hopi} The hump-backed flute-player kachina, who is often portrayed in the form of a grasshopper, carrying the seeds of corn, beans and squash beneath his wing-covers. See *kachina*.

**Lacandon Maya** (Lah-kahn-dohn´ My´-uh). The Mayan people of the highland jungles of Chiapas Province in eastern Mexico.

**maize** (mays). {Taino} Corn. From *mahiz*.

**Mandan** (Man´-dan). Earth-lodge-dwelling agricultural people of the Great Plains. Today they are one of the Three Affiliated Tribes at Fort Berthold, North Dakota.

**mano** (mah´-no). A handheld stone used to grind grains and other food items against a metate.

**Massachusett** (Mass-ah-chu´-set). Algonquin-speaking people of New England whose homeland was in the area of Massachusetts Bay. The literal meaning, from the word *massa-adchu-es-et*, is "About the Great Hill."

**Maxidiwiac** (Mah-shee´ dih-wee´-ak). {Hidatsa} 1839–1920s. Buffalo Bird Woman. Hidatsa woman whose traditional horticultural knowledge is recorded in *Buffalo Bird Woman's Garden.*

**Maya** (My´-uh). A Native people of Middle America with large populations in western Mexico, Belize and Guatemala. The Maya possessed a sophisticated urban culture, with monumental cities, for centuries before the coming of Europeans. Their techniques of rainforest agriculture are still the most effective and sustainable for their region of the world.

**metate** (meh´-tahd-eh). {Nahuatl} Large concave stone on which maize and other grains are ground. From *metlatl.*

**Milpa** (Mill´-pah). {Maya} A rainforest garden of the Maya of Middle America, which uses the sophisticated techniques of swidden agriculture, including crop rotation, companion planting, fertilizing and mulching.

**Mohawk** (Mo´-hawk). {Haudenosaunee} The Haudenosaunee (Iroquois) people whose traditional homeland is the Mohawk Valley of present-day New York. From the Abenaki word *maquak*, meaning "those who are afraid." See *Kanienkahageh.*

**Muskogee** (Mus-ko´-jee). The people most frequently referred to as the Creek. The name *Creek* probably derives from the fact that white traders encountered their villages along streams from the Atlantic coast of Georgia through central Alabama. One of the Five Civilized Tribes. The exact meaning of *Muskogee* is unknown.

**Nahua** (Nah-wa´). Group of peoples in central Mexico who share the Nahuatl language and certain social customs. Although they referred to themselves as "Mexica," the common name of "Aztec" comes from Aztlan, a semimythical location from which the Mexica traveled before coming to the Valley of Mexico, where a great city was constructed on the islands in Lake Texcoco.

**Nanepashemet** (Nah-neh-pah´-sheh-met). {Wampanoag} 1954–1995. Wampanoag scholar and lecturer who worked as Native advisor and researcher at Plimoth Plantation in Massachusetts.

**Narragansett** (Nayr-ah-gahn´-sett). The "People of the Small Bay" were one of the larger and more important tribal nations of the area now known as New England. Present-day Rhode Island approximates the traditional territory of the Narragansetts, who drew on the sea and the forests, as well as farming, for their subsistence.

**Navajo** (Nah´-vah-ho). See *Diné.*

**Neh tsoi** (Neht soy´). {Maya} "Very good."

**nokehick** (no-ke´-hik).{Narragansett} Parched cornmeal, which is sometimes used to make a type of corn cake, today known as Johnnycakes. Also known as *noohkik.*

**Nuxi Balam** (New-shee´ Bah´-lahm). {Maya}. Farmer jaguar.

**olla** (oh´-lah). {Latin} From *aulla*, meaning "pot." An earthenware jar.

**Omaha** (Oh´-ma-ha). {Siouan} Relatives of the Sioux, the Omaha live in present-day northeastern Nebraska. From *U´mon´ha*, meaning "those going against the wind."

**Onenha** (Oh-nen´-hah). {Tuscarora} Corn, "the sustainer."

**Onondaga** (On-un-dah´-gah). {Haudenosaunee} "The Place Among the Hills." One of the five original Haudenosaunee nations. Onondaga is the place where the Great Pine Tree, the emblem of their League of Peace, is symbolically planted. The contemporary city of Syracuse, New York, is on Onondaga land and a large part of the city is still leased from the Onondaga Nation. See *Haudenosaunee*.

**O'odham** (Ōh-ōh´-dum). {Papago} "The People." Southwestern Native people of the Sonora Desert region of present-day Arizona and Mexico.

**Papago** (Pah´-pah-gō). Desert farmers of the Sonora. From *papah o´odham*, meaning "Bean People." See *Tohono O´odham*.

**Pawnee** (Paw-nee´). A people of the northern Great Plains who call themselves *Chahiksihohiks*, meaning "Men of Men." The name *Pawnee*, whose exact source is uncertain, may mean "Hunters" or "Horn."

**piki** (pee´-key). {Hopi} A blue cornbread wafer.

**Pima** (Pee´-mah). Sophisticated farmers of the Sonora Desert of present-day Arizona and Mexico. The name appears to have originated from a phrase used to answer the many questions the early Spanish asked them: *Pi nyi maach*, meaning "I don´t know." See *Akimel O´odham*.

**Pueblo** (Pweb´-lō). {Spanish} "Town." The word refers to a number of "town-dwelling" Native peoples in the Southwest, especially along the Rio Grande, who live in large adobe buildings like apartment complexes.

**Qoyawayma, Sevenka.** {Hopi} ?–1951. Hopi woman of New Oraibi, Third Mesa, Arizona.

**Quechan** (Kweh´-chan). A Native people who live along the Yuma River in Arizona. Their name for themselves is *Quechan* or *Euqchan*. They are also known as *Yuman*.

**Sekatau, Ella** (See´-kah-tow). {Narragansett} 1928– . Dr. Ella Sekatau, DHL, ethnohistorian and cultural education consultant for the Narragansett Indian Tribe, is also a political activist and an accomplished artisan well known for her fine weavings and embroidery. Her historical research was instrumental in bringing about the recognition of the Narragansett by the U.S. government in 1983.

**Siksika** (Seek´-see-ka). A people of the northern plains, especially Montana and Alberta Province. They called themselves *Siksika* meaning "black foot," which refers to their black-dyed moccasins.

**Squanto** (Skwahn´-toh). Wampanoag man who was kidnapped in 1614 or 1615 by the British slave trader Thomas Hunt during a raid on the Wampanoag village of Patuxet. In Europe, Squanto escaped slavery, learned to speak fluent English and eventually returned home to a deserted village that was devastated by slave trading and diseases. Still, beginning in March of 1621, Squanto, individuals from the Massachusett and other local peoples taught the newly arrived Plimoth colonists how to survive by growing corn, beans and squash, including pumpkins. The colonists were from European cities and towns and did not know how to raise European crops.

**succotash** (suck´-oh-tash). {Narragansett} A dish made of beans, squash and corn boiled together.

**Taino** (Ty´-noh). Original Native people of the Caribbean islands.

**Taos** (Tah´-ohs). One of the Pueblo villages along the Rio Grande in New Mexico.

**Teosinte** (Ta-yo´-sin-tee). {Nahuatl} A large grass found in Middle America that is regarded as the ancestor of corn. From *teotl*, meaning "god," and *centli*, meaning "an ear of corn."

**Tewa** (Tey´-wah). Those Pueblo people who speak the Tewa language. Other languages spoken by the various Pueblos include Keresan and Towa.

**Three Sisters.** {Iroquois} A term used by the Haudenosaunee to refer to Corn, Beans and Squash—considered the Three Maidens who help to sustain the people by providing them food.

**Tohono O'odham** (To-ho´-no Oh-oh´-dum). {Papago} "Desert People." See *Papago*.

**Tuscarora** (Tus-kah-roh´-rah). {Iroquois} "Shirt-wearers." The Sixth Nation of the Iroquois League, who were taken in by the Oneidas after being driven from their homelands in North Carolina in the 1700s. See *Haudenosaunee*.

**Tutelo** (Tu-tah´-lo). A now-vanished Native nation of North Carolina and Virginia that was partially absorbed by the Iroquois after being dispossessed of their homeland.

**Wakanda** (Wah-kon´-dah). {Arikara} "The Great Mystery," The Creator.

**Wampanoag** (Wom-pah-nō´-ag). "Dawn Earth People" or "People of the East." Often translated as "People of the First Light." Their original homeland is the area now known as eastern Rhode Island, Cape Cod and coastal Massachussetts. The Pilgrims landed on Wampanoag land in 1620 and were saved by them from starvation. The largest Wampanoag communities today are found in the area of Martha´s Vineyard and Nantucket.

**Yuman** (Yoo´-mun). See *Quechan*.

**Zuni** (Zoo´-nee). A Pueblo people of New Mexico who call themselves *Ashiwi*, meaning "The Flesh." The exact meaning of *Zuni* is unknown.

# Index

# About the Authors

## Michael J. Caduto

*Photo by John Sheldon*

Michael J. Caduto has been a gardener and lover of plants since he was a child. The peace of mind and centering influence he finds in the garden are akin to his experience of the natural world. In many of his educational programs he has taught children the basics of ecological gardening as an important aspect of their relationship with Earth, and as a way of better understanding their role in the Circles of Life. Michael studied agriculture at the undergraduate level at the University of Rhode Island and has worked on several small farms. He has also published a number of articles in *Organic Gardening* magazine. Michael lives and gardens in Vermont.

Michael is an author, storyteller, ecologist, educator, poet, singer and songwriter. In 1984 he founded P.E.A.C.E.®, Programs for Environmental Awareness and Cultural Exchange, to promote understanding, awareness, appreciation and stewardship as the basis for building a harmonious relationship between people and Earth and among the cultures of North America. Michael, who is of Italian ancestry, has worked closely with people from many Native North American cultures for the last fifteen years and actively supports Native visions of Earth stewardship. He travels from his home in Vermont throughout the world, presenting environmental and cultural performances, speeches and workshops for children, teachers, naturalists, families and conferences. Michael's first collection of original music, called *All One Earth: Songs for the Generations,* was released in spring 1995 on compact disc and audiocassette.

Michael has been awarded the New York State Outdoor Education Association's Art and Literary Award and, in 1992, received the New England Regional Environmental Educator Award. His music has won a Popular Award from ASCAP (American Society of Composers, Authors and Publishers). Michael's awards for writing include an American Booksellers "Pick of the List" Award (1991) and the 1992 Association of Children's Booksellers Choice Award. He holds a B.S. in Natural Resources from the University of Rhode Island and an M.S. in Natural Resources/Environmental Education from the University of Michigan. He serves as a Senior Education Fellow with the Atlantic Center for the Environment in Ipswich, Massachusetts.

His writing has appeared in dozens of books and he has published more than one hundred articles in national and international magazines such as *Organic Gardening, Nature Study, Ranger Rick's NatureScope* and *Journal of Environmental Education.* He has written and co-authored eight books. Michael is the creator and co-author of the national bestsellers *Keepers of the Earth* (Fulcrum, 1988), *Keepers of the Animals* (Fulcrum, 1991), *Keepers of the Night* (Fulcrum, 1994) and *Keepers of Life* (Fulcrum, 1994). He also wrote *Pond and Brook* (University Press of New England, 1990) and *A Guide on Environmental Values Education* (UNESCO, 1985), available in English and Spanish.

# Joseph Bruchac

Joseph Bruchac lives with his wife, Carol, in the Adirondack Mountain foothill town of Greenfield Center, New York, in the same house where his maternal grandparents raised him. Much of his writing draws on that land and his Abenaki heritage. Although his American Indian heritage is only part of an ethnic background that includes Slovak and English blood, those Native roots are the ones by which he has been most nourished. He and his two grown sons, James and Jesse, have worked extensively on projects involving the preservation of Abenaki culture, language and traditional Native skills. With James, Jesse and his sister Marge, he performs traditional and contemporary Abenaki music as a member of the Dawn Land Singers.

*Photo by Mike Greenlar*

He holds a B.A. from Cornell University, an M.A. in Literature and Creative Writing from Syracuse University and a Ph.D. in Comparative Literature from the Union Institute of Ohio. His work as an educator includes eight years of directing a college program for Skidmore College inside a maximum security prison. He has been a visiting scholar or writer-in-residence at a number of schools over the past decade including Hamilton College, Columbia University and the State University of New York at Albany. With his wife, Carol, he is the founder and co-director of the Greenfield Review Literary Center and the Greenfield Review Press. He has edited a number of highly praised anthologies of contemporary poetry and fiction, including *Songs from this Earth on Turtle's Back, Breaking Silence* (winner of an American Book Award) and *Returning the Gift.*

His poems, articles and stories have appeared in over five hundred publications, from *American Poetry Review, Cricket* and *Aboriginal Voices* to *National Geographic, Parabola* and *Smithsonian Magazine.* He has authored more than sixty books for adults and children, including *Thirteen Moons on Turtle's Back* (co-authored with Michael London), which was chosen as a 1993 Notable Children's Book in the Language Arts and an IRA Young Adults and Teachers Choice. His more recent books include two novels for adult readers, *Dawn Land* (1993) and *Long River* (1995); and two collections of short stories for young readers, *Dog People* (1995) from Fulcrum Publishing and *The Boy Who Lived With the Bears* (1995) from HarperCollins. He has written picture books for children, including *The Great Ball Game* (1994) and *The Story of the Milky Way* (co-authored with Gayle Ross, 1995) from Dial; *Gluskabe and the Four Wishes* (1995) from Cobblehill; and *A Boy Called Slow* (1995) and *The Earth Under Sky Bear's Feet* (1995) from Philomel Books. New books in 1996 include *Children of the Longhouse* (Dial), a novel for young readers; *Between Earth and Sky* (Harcourt), a picture book illustrated by Thomas Locker; and *Roots of Survival* (Fulcrum), a collection of essays.

He is the winner of a Rockefeller Humanities Fellowship, an NEA Writing Fellowship for Poetry, the Cherokee Nation Prose Award and the Hope S. Dean Award for Notable Achievement in Children's Literature from the Foundation for Children's Literature. In 1993 he was given the Benjamin Franklin Award as "Person of the Year" by the Publishers Marketing Association. His most recent honors include the Scientific American Young Readers Book Award in 1995 for *The Story of the Milky Way* and a 1995 Parents'

Choice Honor Award for *Dog People*. In 1996 his book *A Boy Called Slow* was chosen as an ALA Notable Book and also won Mountains & Plains Booksellers Association Regional Book Award for Children's Writing. In 1996 he was given the Knickerbocker Award for Juvenile Literature by the New York State Library Association.

In addition to performing with the Dawn Land Singers, his most active work in the performing arts over the last two decades has been in the field of storytelling. He has been a storyteller-in-residence for Native American organizations and schools throughout the continent, including the Institute of Alaska Native Arts and the Onondaga Nation School. As a professional teller of the traditional tales of the Adirondacks and the Native peoples of the Northeastern Woodlands, Joe Bruchac has performed widely in Europe and throughout the United States and has been a featured performer at such events as the British Storytelling Festival, the National Storytelling Festival in Jonesboro, Tennessee, the Stone Soup Storytelling Festival and The Bay Area Storytelling Festival.